Mysteries of the Sea

Doug Perrine

PUBLICATIONS INTERNATIONAL, LTD.

Doug Perrine is a full-time writer and photographer specializing in marine wildlife. He has years of experience working with sharks, whales, and dolphins, both as a researcher and a photographer. His underwater photo library, Innerspace Visions, has been published in dozens of books and hundreds of magazines, including *National Geographic Traveler*, *Smithsonian*, *Time*, *Newsweek*, *Ocean Realm*, and *Outside*. He has authored the book *Sharks* and has served as consultant for the Discovery Channel and National Geographic Society. He holds a masters degree in biology and living resources with a specialty in fishery science from the University of Miami.

Louis Weber, C.E.O.
Publications International, Ltd.
7373 North Cicero Avenue
Lincolnwood, Illinois 60646

Manufactured in U.S.A.

8 7 6 5 4 3 2 1

ISBN: 0-7853-2430-5

Library of Congress Catalog Card Number: 97-66699

Photo credits:

Front cover: **Jonathan Bird/Oceanic Research Group:** (right center); **Deborah Fugitt:** (left center); **Norbert Wu:** (background).

Back cover: **Innerspace Visions:** Doug Perrine: (center); Mark Strickland: (top).

Animals Animals: E.R. Degginger: 38; Shane Moore: 185; **Frank S. Balthis:** 51, 66, 93 (bottom), 137, 144-145, 276 (top), 277; **Bob Cranston:** 208; **Ned DeLoach/New World Publications:** 78; **FPG International:** Lee Foster: 127; Thayer Syme: 212-213; Karl & Jill Wallin: 176 (bottom), 211; **David B. Fleetham:** 112, 229; **Scott**

Frier/Ocean Stock: 245, 257; **Deborah Fugitt:** 29, 60, 83, 196, 206, 223 (bottom), 240, 256 (top), 267, 274; **Al Giddings Images, Inc.:** 258; **Howard Hall Photography:** 52, 129 (bottom), 141, 142, 186, 226; Michele Hall: table of contents (center), 220, 243 (top); **Paul Humann:** 65, 114, 218 (bottom); **Innerspace Visions:** Brandon D. Cole: 45, 46-47; Andrea & Antonella Ferrari: 204; Howard Hall: 171; Richard Herrmann: 40; Marilyn Kazmers: 179, 217, 224 (top); Avi Klapfer: 19 (top); Hiroya Minakuchi: 133; Mike Nolan: 262; Doug Perrine: table of contents (top & bottom), 13, 15, 18, 20, 22, 23, 24, 25, 27, 30, 32, 34, 35, 36, 49, 54-55, 56, 57, 67 (top), 69, 76, 77 (bottom), 79, 88, 106, 107, 110, 116, 119 (bottom), 122, 123, 138, 154, 155, 156, 157, 160, 161, 162, 163, 167, 168, 172, 176 (top), 177, 180, 181, 184, 189, 191, 194, 195 (top), 201, 209, 210, 216, 219, 225, 230-231, 248, 249, 254, 255, 256 (bottom), 259, 266, 268 (bottom), 278, 281, 282, 283, 284, 287, 293, 295, 300-301; Mike Schmale: 87; Marty Snyderman: 149; Walt Stearns: 147; Mark Strickland: 37, 305; **Charles Mazel:** 235, 236; **Oceanic Research Group:** Jonathan Bird: 64, 84, 151, 164, 227, 285; Millhouser: 119 (top); **Gregory Ochocki:** 251; **Oxford Scientific Films:** Doug Allan: 93 (top); Max Gibbs: 187; Rodger Jackman: 101 (top); Tony Martin: 92; Peter Parks: 73; **Jeffrey L. Rotman:** 182, 253; **John G. Shedd Aquarium:** 43, 44; **Brian Skerry:** 129 (top), 140; **Marty Snyderman:** 6 (bottom), 10, 12, 14, 17, 26, 33, 48, 53, 70, 77 (top), 81, 82, 89, 90, 113, 117, 124, 134, 139, 146, 153, 169 (top), 192, 214, 215, 224 (bottom), 241, 244 (top), 260-261, 268 (top), 279, 280, 299; **Tom Stack & Associates:** 42, 173 (bottom), 221; Mike Bacon: 4, 59, 178 (bottom), 193, 223 (top), 232; D. Holden Bailey: 239; David B. Fleetham: 7, 115, 152, 199, 247, 294; Jeff Foott: 100; Garoutle Bay Islands: 195 (bottom); Kerry T. Givens: 148; J. Lotter Gurling: 166; Larry Lipsky: 159; Gary Milburn: 234, 286; Randy Morse: 165, 265; Michael Nolan: 252; Brian Parker: 103, 228, 276 (bottom); Patrice: 143, 269; Ed Robinson: 16, 120, 222; Rick Sammon: 244 (bottom), 292; Dave Watts: 273; **Mark Strickland/Oceanic Impressions:** 243 (bottom), 296, 297; **Andrew G. Wood:** 121, 126, 198, 218 (top), 233; **Norbert Wu:** 5, 6 (top), 8-9, 11, 19 (bottom), 21, 28, 31, 39, 41, 61, 62, 63, 67 (bottom), 68, 71, 72, 85, 86, 91, 94, 96, 97, 101 (bottom), 102, 104-105, 108-109, 111, 118, 125, 128, 132, 135, 136, 158, 169 (bottom), 173 (top), 174-175, 178 (top), 183, 188, 190, 197, 202, 203, 207, 237, 238, 242, 246, 264, 271, 291, 298; Mo Yung Productions: Marjorie Bank: 205; Brandon D. Cole: 98, 99, 130-131, 288-289; Mark Conlin: 80; Bruce Rasner: 303; Ken Smith: 302; James Watt: 74-75, 95, 150, 272; **Jill Yager/Dennis Williams:** 304.

Contents

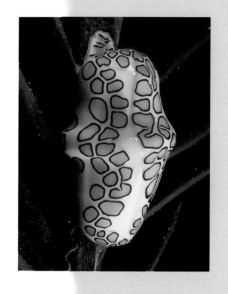

The Blue World

In 1996 new evidence was discovered that life may once have existed on Mars, fueling a new wave of speculation that we may some day encounter intelligent beings from elsewhere in the universe. The public fascination with this possibility has spawned a multibillion dollar industry in science fiction books, movies, television shows, and video games.

Amidst the hoopla over hypothetical extraterrestrials, we have largely ignored the millions of alien species right here on our own planet, including some that are highly intelligent. In fact, the largest brains on Earth, and perhaps in the universe, belong to mysterious creatures living in a hostile environment—an environment we cannot survive in without special equipment similar to that used for space travel. These living wonders, the whales, include the

Opposite: Coral reef in the Red Sea
Below: Moorish idols and butterflyfish

5

Above: *Moray eels* Right: *Lacy scorpionfish.*

largest animal that has ever lived, bigger than any dinosaur—the blue whale. In spite of having killed thousands of them, and having driven several species to extinction or near-extinction, we know extremely little of the lives of these animals and of the oceans that nourish them.

The sea covers 71 percent of the earth's surface and comprises 95 percent of its biosphere, or living space. Yet we know less about the bottom of the ocean than we do about the surface of the moon. The more we learn about the oceans, the more obvious it becomes how little we know. A number of new species of marine plants and animals are discovered every year and, quite frequently, entirely new types of organisms are discovered.

Animals are classified by scientists into a hierarchical system of categories. The largest category is the phylum—an extremely broad grouping. For example, all animals with spinal chords, including the vertebrates—humans and other mammals, fish, amphibians, reptiles, and birds—plus the hemichordates and the tunicates, belong to the phylum Chordata. In 1996 scientists an-

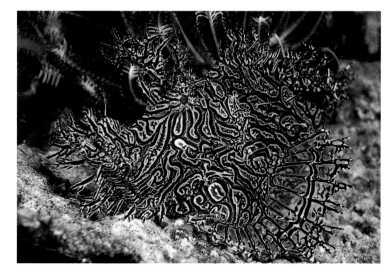

Above: *Whitetip reef shark*

nounced the discovery of a marine organism so unlike other animals that it needed a new phylum. Discoveries of new species and new groups of creatures are much less frequent on land, where less is hidden from us.

Hollywood has not totally ignored the curious and often bizarre creatures to be found in the ocean. Sometimes they are used as the basis for imaginary space aliens or monsters. However, the imagination of scriptwriters rarely matches the incredible truth about the lives of the real aliens—aliens from inner space, the blue world that begins at our shoreline.

It would require an entire encyclopedia to summarize even the meager knowledge we already have of life in the ocean. This book will merely touch on a variety of interesting topics and unanswered questions concerning this mysterious realm and the extraordinary beings inhabiting it.

Odd Couples

In delicate shades of lavender, violet, fuchsia, chartreuse, and cream, the tentacles of sea anemones sway in the current like the attractive flowers for which they are named. But these are not plants—they are deadly predators with a taste for the flesh of fish. Their beautifully colored tentacles are loaded with poisoned harpoon capsules that are triggered by the touch of a prey organism. The unsuspecting fish who blunders into the arms of one of these Medusas is assaulted by the simultaneous

9

A sea anemone may host a whole community of symbiotic organisms, such as these anemonefish and porcelain crabs.

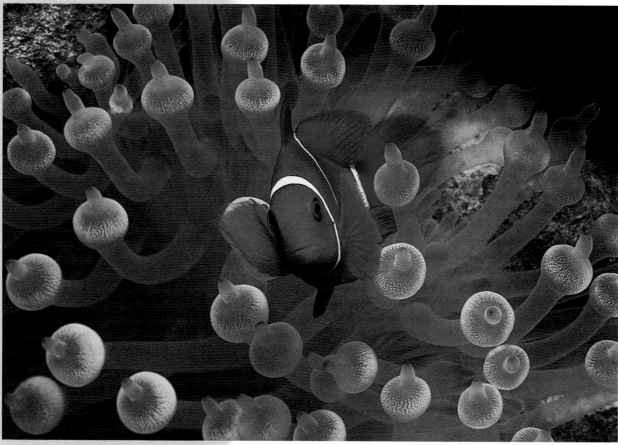

A spine-cheeked anemonefish hides among the tentacles of a bulb-tipped anemone. The fish may eat scraps from the anemone's meals as well as gaining protection from its tentacles. It may also aid the anemone by luring prey within the range of its deadly tentacles.

firing of thousands of these capsules. Tiny tubules coiled inside explode outward, penetrating the victim's flesh and delivering a paralyzing venom. The arms fold around the weakly struggling fish and draw it rapidly into the anemone's mouth.

Yet while this is occurring, other fish may be swimming freely among the tentacles of the sea anemone. Undaunted by its weaponry, anemonefish form a unique partnership with the anemone. The fish find shelter from other predators in the arms of the anemone and sometimes eat scraps from the anemone's meals. The anemonefish sometimes return the favor by bringing, or luring, food to the anemone. But how do they avoid being stung and eaten themselves? Scientists puzzled over this question for decades.

A DEADLY EMBRACE AND A MAGIC COAT. Scientists found that if an anemonefish was separated from its host anemone for a long enough period of time, it would lose its immunity and would be stung when it was reunited with the anemone. But by exposing itself a little at a time to the anemone, the anemonefish could gradually reacquire its immunity. The protection came from the coat of mucus covering the fish. But is the fish able to manufacture its own "bulletproof jacket," or does it obtain protection by rubbing mucus off the anemone itself, fooling the anemone into thinking it's touching one of its own tentacles?

If an anemonefish is taken away from its host and placed instead with an artificial anemone, it still requires time to reacclimate when returned to the real anemone. But this period is much shorter than for a fish placed in an empty tank during separation from its host. Apparently the fish is able to produce some of the protective material but requires input from the anemone to complete the job. What does the fish obtain by touching the anemone, and how does this protect it from being stung? This is one of many mysteries surrounding the curious partnerships formed between various sorts of marine organisms.

PARTNERSHIPS. Like creatures on

land, no marine creature lives in isolation but is rather a part of an ecosystem with many interconnected parts. Evolution may have been proceeding in the ocean for at least twice as long as life has existed on land, and environmental disturbances tend to be less extreme in the sea than ashore, possibly with fewer mass extinctions. For these reasons, an even more elaborate network of interrelationships has evolved underwater than in the terrestrial wilderness. In many cases one or both partners have become completely dependent upon the other and

An anemonefish rubs against the tentacles of its host anemone. The fish must maintain regular contact with its host or it will lose its immunity to the tentacles' sting.

cannot survive alone. Some partnerships benefit both members; this relationship is known as mutualism. In other cases one partner benefits more than the other; this is called commensalism. One partner may even harm the other member (parasitism). All of these sorts of relationships are known as symbiosis, from the Greek word for "living together."

MUTUAL PROTECTION.

A variety of small shrimp and crabs also are found living in many sea anemones. These diminutive crustaceans seem to have less immunity to the sting of the anemone than the anemonefish does. Their protection may be merely the coat of armor they wear as a shell. These creatures prefer to reside underneath the anemone and on the lower parts of the tentacles, generally avoiding the tips of the tentacles, where the stinging harpoons are clustered. In some cases, the shrimp help to protect the anemone, just as the anemone protects the shrimp.

In the Caribbean, corkscrew anemones commonly shelter tiny Pederson's shrimp and one or two much larger and more aggressive red snapping shrimp, or "pistol shrimp." When a large object, such as a diver's hand, approaches the anemone, the snapping shrimp frequently marches out to confront it with claws raised. In one experiment the snapping shrimp were removed from their host anemones; the anemones disappeared from the reef within a few weeks.

In the Pacific Ocean, some hard corals have small crabs living among their branches that serve a similar protective role. These crabs will attack organisms that threaten their home, even much larger organisms than the crabs themselves. Crown-of-thorns sea stars, for example, eat corals and periodically occur in plague proportions.

A sea anemone may host from one to dozens of tiny shrimp, which may share the anemone with other symbionts.

During invasions of them, corals with resident crabs survive, while those without crabs do not.

DANCING IN THE JAWS OF DEATH. Many anemone shrimp maintain symbiotic relationships not only with the host anemone but also with a variety of fishes. These fish visit the anemone specifically to avail themselves of the services of the shrimp. The shrimp are often decorated with long, white antennae, which they wave back and forth while doing a little jig near the anemone. The dance and waving antennae advertise to passing fish that the shrimp is available to

Corkscrew sea anemones often shelter a red snapping shrimp, or pistol shrimp, which is usually hidden behind the tentacles. But when something threatens the anemone, the shrimp comes out waving its powerful claws and sometimes snapping them to drive the intruder away.

The cleaning shrimp waves its long, white antennae to attract customers for parasite removal. This shrimp is transparent, but it appears red-violet because of the color of the anemone tentacles behind it.

accept clients. The service offered is parasite removal. A fish wishing to be serviced stops and adopts a rather unusual posture, often with the head up or down and the mouth and gill plates flared open. This signals the shrimp that the fish is ready to accept its services. The shrimp hops aboard and clambers about the fish, entering even the most delicate areas, including the mouth and gills, and even marching right across the eyeball, picking off and eating smaller crustaceans that infest the fish, removing bits of dead skin and diseased tissue as well.

Small fish also often perform this cleaning service. Some of these cleaner fish are juveniles of many

Treacherous Tricksters

Considering the continuous brutal struggle for survival in the ocean, it is not surprising that some organisms have found a way to take advantage of this mutual relationship between cleaners and their clients. The saber-toothed blenny is a small fish almost identical in appearance to the common cleaner wrasse, which is the most abundant and widespread cleaning fish in the Indo-Pacific. The blenny also mimics the swimming dance that the cleaner wrasse uses to attract clients. However, a fish approaching to be cleaned discovers an important difference between the wrasse and the blenny. The wrasse uses tiny comblike teeth to manicure the skin of its clients. When the blenny opens its mouth, it reveals not these tiny teeth, but a pair of oversize fangs, which it uses to rip off a morsel of flesh from the unsuspecting fish. The blenny then dashes to the shelter of the reef before the astonished victim can recover and retaliate.

species that as adults alter their diet, behavior, and appearance. Some fish change color when they are being cleaned or when they wish to be cleaned. Skin parasites that were perfectly camouflaged against the fish's normal coloration suddenly stand out against the changed background and are easily located by the cleaners.

Locations where the cleaning organisms reside are known as cleaning stations. They are usually set up at prominent reef landmarks, such as an anemone or a high coral head. The relationship is of mutual benefit—the cleaner organism gets a meal while the host gets its parasites removed.

A number of cleaner shrimp service a Nassau grouper parked at a cleaning station. The shrimp hanging upside down from the grouper's upper lip is carrying a clutch of eggs on her abdomen.

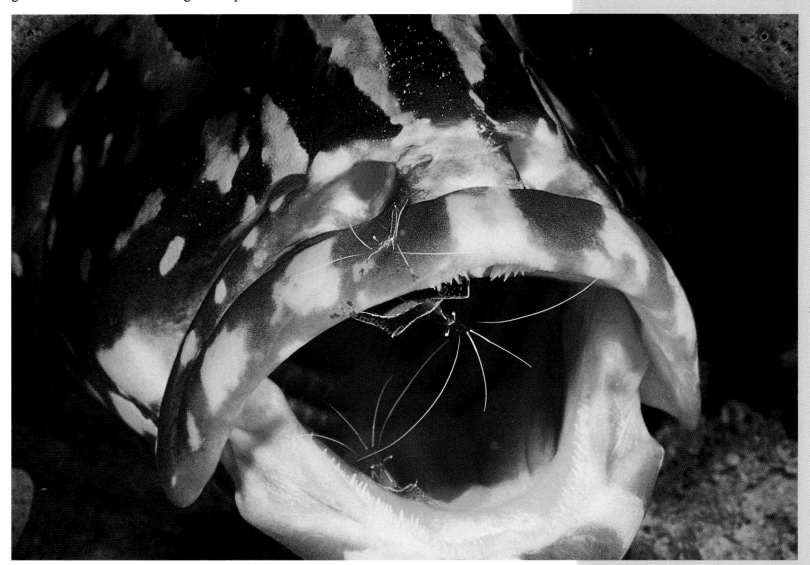

This exchange may be not merely beneficial but essential to the host fish. Where scientists have experimented by removing cleaner organisms from a reef, the fish population has declined drastically shortly afterward. Cleaner fish are often the same size or smaller than the prey of the fish they service. However, the larger fish resist the temptation to take advantage of an easy meal while the cleaner is working inside the larger fish's mouth. This remarkable restraint shows the importance of the cleaners to the fish. A cleaning session can end prematurely when the client swallows and swims away, but such incidents are very rare indeed.

In addition to shrimps and fishes, crabs, worms, and even birds have been observed to function as cleaner organisms. Ocean sunfish, or mola molas, sometimes float on their sides on the ocean surface, and seagulls alight on them and pick off their parasites. Cleaning relationships are ubiquitous in the ocean and involve organisms from the smallest to the largest. Spiny sea urchins are cleaned by small cardinalfish, which hide within the spines of the urchin, finding protection from predators in their pincushionlike home.

FREE LAWN SERVICE AND FAST FOOD DELIVERY. Sea turtles take advantage of cleaning services, not only for parasite removal, but also for shell maintenance. This service is performed by herbivorous fishes such as tangs.

Above: *The Hawaiian cleaner wrasse is a species endemic to the Hawaiian Islands, meaning that it evolved there and occurs nowhere else. This wrasse is cleaning a larger wrasse of a different species.*
Opposite: *A colorful grouper in the South Pacific opens its mouth to accept the services of a cleaner wrasse.*

When the turtle glides up to the cleaning station, the fish swarm over its shell, grazing on the algae that grow on the shell and reduce the turtle's hydrodynamic efficiency as it swims. Slow-moving manatees also can develop coats of algae on their backs, and they attract plant-eating fishes that graze on the mobile "lawn."

Even large sharks must inhibit their predatory instincts at times to take advantage of the cleaning services that seem to be necessary for survival. Sharks are at a disadvantage, though. Many bony fishes have air bladders to give them buoyancy. The shark, a cartilaginous fish, has no air bladder; sharks must continually swim to keep from sinking. Whereas a few sharks, such as the Caribbean

Cleaning relationships do not always involve parasite removal. These herbivorous convict tangs are grazing the algae off the shell of a green sea turtle. The algae may reduce the hydrodynamic efficiency of the turtle.

Left: *This scalloped hammerhead is being cleaned by king angelfish at a seamount. These sharks feed in deeper water, and visiting the cleaning stations may be an important reason to come to the seamounts.* Below: *Whitetip reef sharks have the ability to pump water across their gills while they are resting on the bottom. Therefore they do not have to swim constantly in order to breathe, as many other sharks do. Thus gobies can service them during extended cleaning sessions while the sharks lie motionless.*

reef shark and whitetip reef shark, are able to rest on the bottom and enjoy the services of cleaner fish while in repose, most species have to get their cleaning on the run.

The presence of cleaning stations may be a major reason why scalloped hammerhead sharks aggregate by day at seamounts, or mountains rising up from the seafloor, some distance from the locations where they feed at night. As the sharks approach the reef, cleaner fish, including king angel-fish and streamer hogfish, swim out to meet them. The hammerheads glide in, slowing to a near stall while the fish climb aboard and swarm over them. Then, just before it begins to sink, with a kick of the tail the shark accelerates back out to the blue water beyond the reef, where it will join the larger school patrolling the seamount and waiting for nightfall.

Giant manta rays often glide into seamounts to utilize the services of the same cleaners that the hammerheads use. The manta's hydrodynamic shape is

A remora hitches a ride on the back of a giant manta ray. The remora attaches by means of a suction disc on top of its head and may attach in an upside-down position, like this one, or right side up on the underside of the host.

remarkably similar to that of a stealth jet, and probably not by coincidence. If a current is running, the manta can actually stop in place while it is being cleaned, even though mantas, like sharks, have no air bladder. Like the airflow over an airplane wing, the current flowing over the manta's wings provides enough lift to keep it from sinking.

UNINVITED GUESTS. Mantas and other large marine animals often carry other associates with them as well—remoras, or suckerfish or sharksuckers. Remoras have a flattened disc on the top of the head equipped with a venetian-blind-like structure that creates a formidable suction to attach themselves to the host organism. Free-swimming remoras will investigate and attempt to attach themselves to almost any large moving object in their vicinity. The attachment is so secure that it is almost impossible to remove the remora. Hawaiians and other native islanders were known to fish for sea turtles by attaching a line to the tail of a remora and throwing it into the ocean near a turtle. When the remora attached itself to the turtle, the turtle could be hauled in by the line attached to the remora. The line would break before the remora would separate from the turtle. Animals without shells, such as mantas and dolphins, can often be seen with marks, bruises, or even open sores caused by the attachment of remoras. They sometimes attach to human divers, who have reported that they can leave a painful bruise.

From examining the stomach contents of remoras, it appears that at least sometimes they do eat the parasites infesting their hosts. But the relationship is much more complex than a simple cleaning association, and many questions are left to be answered. In addition to consuming external parasites, remoras have been seen eating scraps from their host's meals, snapping up organisms stirred up by the host's foraging, and even dining on the host's waste products during defecation. They are obviously not very thorough in their parasite removal services,

The surface of the attachment disc on the top of a remora's head contains venetian-blind-like ridges, which create a suction holding the remora tightly to its host. The discs can leave marks that look like sneaker footprints on the tough skin of manta rays and open sores on dolphins.

A remora clings tightly to the side of a dolphin as it performs a high jump. An attempt to dislodge remoras may be one reason that dolphins jump.

because mantas with multiple remoras visit cleaning stations in order to be serviced by jacks and angelfish as well. A manta with a pair of remoras may be relatively parasite-free, but the remoras themselves are often covered with "fish lice" (parasitic crustaceans). A mystery is why they don't eat each others' lice.

If remoras perform the valuable service of parasite removal, one would expect them to be welcomed by the host in spite of any discomfort from the attachment and increased drag during swimming. In fact, they appear to be well tolerated by a number of hosts. But many animals seem to find the remoras bothersome and attempt to dislodge them through various means. Parrotfish, in particular, seem to find remoras intolerable. A parrotfish with even a small sharksucker—a type of remora—attached to it spends a lot of time writhing around trying to scrape the pest off against the reef. Whales, dolphins, and mantas and other types of rays breach, or leap clear of the water to reenter with a resounding splash. One reason proposed for this is to dislodge remoras. People have observed that dolphins with remoras tend to breach more often than those without remoras. However, dolphins are very social animals and are known to help one another when in distress. They are also fish eaters. One wonders why dolphins don't simply eat each other's remoras.

Sharks appear to tolerate remoras without distress. Very large sharks, such as whale sharks, may be accompanied by correspondingly large numbers of remoras. When danger threatens, the remoras often seek shelter in any available opening, including the gill slits, the spiracle (an opening behind the gill slits), and the cloaca (the combined genital/anal opening). It may be that sharks are less annoyed by suckerfish because the sharks' tough skin is less susceptible to damage from the powerful suckers.

In at least one species, however, the remoras sometimes perform an additional valuable function. Some sharks, unlike bony fish, do not lay eggs, but give live birth, utilizing a placental system similar to that of mammals. Lemon sharks return to shallow lagoons and estuaries like those in which they themselves were born in order to deliver their pups. As a pregnant lemon shark nears term, she collects an increasing number of sharksuckers. As the dozen or so pups in the litter emerge from the womb, they sometimes have difficulty breaking the umbil-

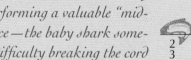

Sharksuckers nip at the umbilical cord as a lemon shark is born. They may be performing a valuable "midwife" service—the baby shark sometimes has difficulty breaking the cord by itself. Of course the sharksuckers are interested only in getting a meal.

Sharksuckers devour the afterbirth as a lemon shark rests on the lagoon floor between the births of a series of pups. The sharksucker at upper right is feeding on the pseudo placenta, which serves a function similar to that of the placenta in mammals.

ical cord, which binds them to the afterbirth. They can be freed by the sharksuckers, which sever the umbilical cords in their frenzy of consuming the afterbirth.

WHO'S FOLLOWING WHOM?

Sharks are often accompanied by a large number of other fish with apparent suicidal tendencies. Some of these fish are only temporary companions, mobbing the shark from behind and striking glancing blows against its flank. Apparently the fish are using the rough skin of the shark—which when dried can be used as sandpaper—as a scratching board to remove their external parasites. Other fish, especially members of the jack family, are longer-term associates. These typically swim in front of or alongside the shark. Pilotfish—a term applying to a number of species of jacks that as juveniles accompany larger fish—swim just in front of the shark's snout. They conserve swimming energy by riding the pressure wave forced ahead of the shark as it swims. Other fish may swim as much as several meters ahead of the shark.

The shark and its entourage appear to move and turn as a single organism, as though their nervous systems were connected through the span of water separating their bodies. To some extent this can be explained by the marvelous lateral line system, a row of nerve cells running the length of a fish's side. They bestow exquisite sensitivity to even minute changes in water pressure, such as those created by the movements of another fish. But this doesn't explain how fish several meters ahead of the shark can respond instantaneously to its changes of direction.

One suggestion is that the shark is actually following the smaller fish, taking advantage of the expanded sensory capabilities of the group. The smaller fish may help the shark to locate food and then benefit by sharing the scraps of its meal. The tiny pilotfish, however, along with the remoras and others that follow behind, beneath, and alongside, are not likely to be of much help in finding food. So it may be that some fish are leading the shark and others are following it. The pilotfish may be following, but in front. Miraculously, they manage to stay right on a shark's nose even when it makes sudden changes in direction. It may be

Golden pilot jacks associate with larger fish, such as this whale shark, only as juveniles. The adults are free-living (and lose the attractive golden color). The jacks ride the pressure wave that the shark pushes ahead of it as it swims. When the shark turns, the jacks turn in unison with it.

more useful to think of the shark and its coterie as a single superorganism, with each member of the group utilizing feedback from all the others.

SCAVENGERS. Jacks frequently associate also with rays, which is not surprising since rays are closely related to sharks. Stingrays foraging for food buried in the sand are often accompanied by a bar jack. Stingrays feed largely on clams and related mollusks, crushing their shells with flat, grinding teeth. By itself, a jack would be unable to get a clam out of the sand, let alone break the shell. But when one is crushed by a stingray, the jack scavenges the bits of clam meat clouding the water around the feeding ray.

A bar jack shadows a stingray as it searches for prey buried in the sand. The stingray can locate buried prey using special organs that detect the electric field created by the muscular activity of the prey organism. The jack does not have this electrical sense.

Bar jacks are normally silver with a blue stripe along the back, but a jack consorting with a stingray nearly always changes its color to a flat black. This is curious because black has no value as camouflage in the areas of white sand where the stingrays feed, and the black color actually makes the jack stand out more obviously. The color may be a warning signal to other members of its species. These jacks, which may school together under other circumstances, become fiercely territorial when they adopt a stingray as a mobile territory and will vigorously drive off any other jack that approaches the ray. Apparently a stingray leaves just enough table scraps to support a single bar jack. Hogfish and a few other sorts of fishes can also sometimes be seen following stingrays in this way.

HOUSEKEEPERS AND GUARDIANS.

In the Indo-Pacific, a number of species of partner gobies share housekeeping with various species of blind shrimp. The shrimp and the goby share a burrow, which is excavated and maintained by the shrimp. From dawn to dusk, the little shrimp can be seen working like a tiny bulldozer pushing debris out of the burrow, while the goby sits at the entrance without lifting a fin to help. The goby, however, contributes

27

An orange-banded partner goby serves as the eyes for its domestic partner. In general, each species of partner goby is found only with a particular species of shrimp.

its keen eyesight to the partnership. Its two raised eyeballs rotate independently, allowing the goby to keep a lookout in all directions at once. Whenever the shrimp ventures out of the burrow, it keeps one antenna in contact with the goby. If the goby turns and dashes into the burrow, the shrimp follows instantly. For many of the species of gobies and shrimp involved in these relationships, one partner is never found independent of the other.

Above: *A red-banded partner goby keeps an alert lookout for predators. Its partner, a blind shrimp, keeps one antenna resting on the goby. If it feels the goby turn for the burrow, it will follow instantly.* Opposite: *The abundance and diversity of life on a coral reef is possible because nutrients are cycled between the reef-dwelling organisms, rather than being lost to the surrounding seawater. This in turn is possible because of intricate relationships between different organisms that have developed over millions of years of evolution.*

INTERNAL GARDENS.

In some cases the relationship between two organisms has evolved to the point where one cannot survive without the other; it is perhaps especially appropriate to think of them as a single compound animal. In the most complete type of symbiosis, one partner may actually live within the tissues of another. Scientists marveled for decades at the mystery of coral reefs. Coral animals use stinging harpoon capsules like those of anemones to capture tiny planktonic animals that float in the current. How could these oases of life thrive in the clear, nutrient-poor waters of the tropics? The small amount of plankton contained there is not enough to support the millions of colonial coral animals, called polyps, that build most of the structure of a reef.

Involuntary Servitude

Some organisms do not associate with their host of their own free will but are merely appropriated by the host to serve its own purposes. The "slave" organism, however, may also benefit from the relationship by receiving protection, transportation, or bits of food from the host's meals. Decorator crabs pick up bits of algae, sponge, hydroids, and other organisms and attach this miscellany to their shells to serve as living camouflage. Sponge crabs cut a large piece of sponge to completely cover their shell and then hide among other sponges. Arrow crabs stick bits of live algae on the spines of their comically extended noses. For the arrow crabs this is not camouflage but a larder. They retrieve the algae to snack on later. Boxer crabs attach live anemones to their claws for defense. The stinging harpoon capsules in the tentacles of the anemones add zing to the crab's punch. Certain types of hermit crabs attach anemones not to their own shells, but to the abandoned shells of marine snails, which the crabs appropriate as mobile homes. When the crab grows too large for its borrowed shell, it locates a larger one and gingerly transfers the anemones to the new home as soon as it moves in.

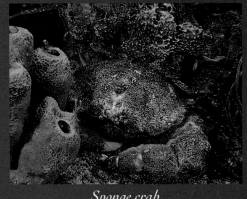

Sponge crab

It seems that the science of agriculture was not invented by our human ancestors but evolved millions of years earlier as a special relationship between coral polyps and minute "plantimals" called zooxanthellae. These microscopic algae are capable of swimming free in the ocean, like animals, but they also contain chlorophyll and produce food from the energy of sunlight, through photosynthesis, like plants.

Plants and animals serve each other well because each can utilize the wastes of the other. Animals require oxygen, which is given off by plants, and release carbon dioxide, which plants require for photosynthesis. Plants also require nitrogen and minerals, which are abundant in animal feces. Plants store energy in carbohydrates, which are an excellent food category for animals. Seawater, however, is a solvent, tending to dilute and carry off nutrients. Corals have solved this problem by capturing the zooxanthellae and "farming" them within their own bodies. Wastes from the corals' metabolism are used directly by the plants, and food from the plants is absorbed directly by the corals. In addition to their own by-products, corals obtain additional fertilizer for their internal gardens by swallowing the feces of fish that pass overhead. At night, when the lack of sunlight to power the photosynthetic machine prevents the zooxanthellae

from producing food, the coral polyps extend their stinging tentacles and capture animal food to supplement their vegetarian diet.

Zooxanthellae can be found free-swimming in plankton and appear to be capable of living indefinitely without their hosts, but many corals cannot survive long without their gardens. When coral reefs come under stress due to high water temperatures or other causes, the corals may expel their zooxanthellae and bleach white. Most of the color of these coral colonies comes from the internal algae—the coral animals are nearly transparent, and their skeletons are white. If the corals do not reacquire zooxanthellae quickly enough when the crisis has passed, they will weaken and die.

Certain other animals, including some anemones, jellyfish, a type of sponge, a worm, and giant clams, also farm zooxanthellae within their bodies. In the clams, the algae occur in spaces within the mantle tissue, coloring the mantle in a variety of different colors. Giant clams can filter-feed through their gills, like other clams, but the nutrition they obtain from their symbiotic algae is essential to their survival. They are found only in shallow water, where they receive enough sunlight to enable the algae to photosynthesize.

Left: The brown portions of this staghorn coral contain living tissue and symbiotic algae. The bleached white portions have lost their algae and are dying or dead. Below: Soft corals, such as the colorful ones in the foreground of this scene, do not contain zooxanthellae. The hard corals in the background do have zooxanthellae, which may assist them in depositing calcium from the seawater into their hard skeletons of calcium carbonate.

FREELOADERS. Some houseguests contribute nothing to their keep. The conchfish resides by day inside the shell of a live conch, coming out at night to feed. When danger threatens, it hides under the conch's mantle. At night the pearlfish, likewise, leaves its host, a sea cucumber, to feed. With its flat, transparent body swaying vertically among blades of sea grass, the pearlfish is almost invisible as it snaps up tiny shrimplike organisms. Not content with the protection of this superb camouflage, however, it never strays far from the slow-moving body of its sluglike host. When feeling threatened, the pearlfish retreats to the rear end of its host and begins to tickle the cucumber's anus with its slender,

A pearlfish feeds in the sand between blades of sea grass. When not feeding, it will assume a vertical position and mimic the blades of grass. If threatened, it will retreat inside the body of its host, a sea cucumber, which is about one foot away.

A sea cucumber may be host to as many as 15 pearlfish, which live inside its digestive tract. Sea cucumbers are related to sea stars, but the five-rayed symmetry is not obvious in the adult.

pointed tail. When the cucumber relaxes its sphincter, the pearlfish slides inside, tail first. Why the sea cucumber should allow this is a mystery.

RASPERS. A symbiont that feeds on or otherwise harms its host is known as a parasite, and the ocean is full of them. A great many animals in the ocean suffer some sort of parasite, and often several different kinds. Parasites may live inside or outside their hosts or visit them only occasionally. Many parasites have evolved elaborate adaptations enabling them to take advantage of specific hosts.

The golden wentletrap snail has a beautiful gold-orange color that enables it to blend in perfectly with the orange cup corals that it hides in. The snail does

A flamingo-tongue snail feeding on the living (purple) tissue of its host, a gorgonian coral. The dark skeleton of the gorgonian is visible where the flesh has been stripped away.

not have to manufacture the pigments, though. It obtains them from the corals themselves. It feeds on them by inserting its long proboscis into the mouth of a coral polyp and rasping away the soft tissues with a toothed organ called a radula. The snail passes these pigments along to its eggs, which it lays among the cup corals, camouflaging them perfectly as well. The snail, then, obtains all its needs in life from the coral, with the host receiving nothing in return.

Many ovulid shells, or allied cowries, also match the color of their hosts perfectly and are almost invisible upon the soft corals they feed on. The beautiful colors and ornate patterns of these marine snails belie their parasitic nature. The flamboyantly patterned flamingo-tongue snail found in the Caribbean also feeds on soft corals. In this case, the host is usually a purple sea fan or purple sea whip. As the snail moves along, it leaves behind a black trail where the purple flesh has been rasped away, revealing the dark skeleton underneath. Oddly, the flamingo-tongue snail does not match its host but covers itself with an orange-splotched mantle, which contrasts vividly with the purple coral. Why does this snail not need to camouflage itself like most other parasites? Perhaps it contains toxins that make it unpalatable to predators, and the bold coloring actually stands out as a warning of its toxicity. Sadly, many of these beautiful shells are collected by divers, who find out to their dismay that the color is all in the flesh of the animal, and the shell itself is a dull creamy white.

BLOODSUCKERS. Another group of snails, the vampire snails, do not have the radula that other snails use to rasp away the tissues of their forage. For years, how these snails fed baffled scientists, especially since nothing identifiable was ever found in their stomachs. The behavior of these animals was very difficult to observe, since by day they lie hidden under rubble in the recesses of the coral

A pair of flamingo-tongue snails on their host, a purple sea fan. The striking pattern on the snails is not on the shell, which is a dull creamy color, but on the fleshy mantle that covers the shell.

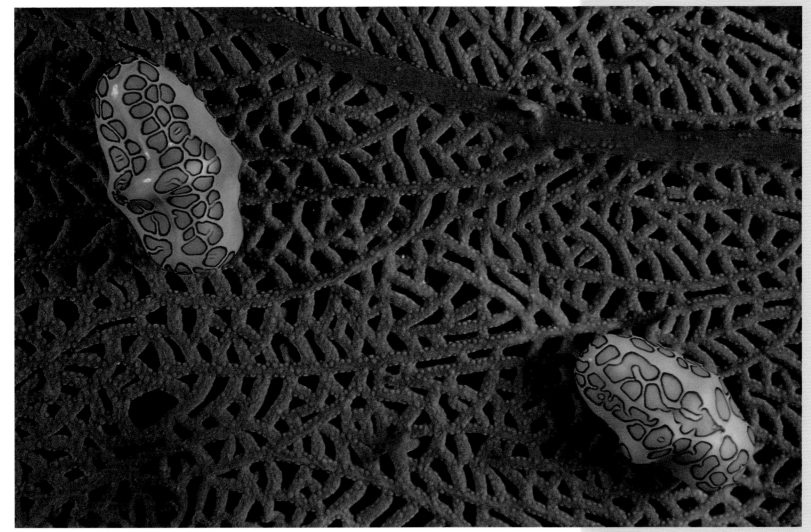

Although its eyes are open, the parrotfish is sound asleep in its coral crevice at night. It is not aware that the feeding tube of a vampire snail has pierced the soft tissues inside of its mouth and is sucking out its body fluids.

reef. Only recently have underwater photographers working at night produced evidence of the actual feeding methods of these diminutive seagoing vampires.

As the reef darkens, parrotfish and other fish active during the day settle into nooks and crannies in the reef to sleep. The vampire snails then come out from under their rocks and begin to hunt. They can sense a sleeping fish from a distance of at least eight inches. The long proboscis coiled within the shell is unsheathed, extends to a length many times that of the snail's body, and begins to search for an opening to the soft tissues of the prey.

Parrotfish have large, hard scales, but they often sleep with their mouths open. The vampire usually extends its proboscis between the formidable jaws of the sleeping fish and into the mouth, where it can pierce the soft tissues of the inside of the mouth, and begins to pump out blood and body fluids. The mucus cocoons that parrotfish often surround

themselves with at night provide no defense against the remorseless snails. They sometimes climb up on the cocoon to get closer to the fish's mouth before piercing first the cocoon and then the fish inside. Sometimes several snails can be seen feeding on the same fish without waking it, with their feeding siphons intertwined, somewhat like the drinking straws of teenagers sharing a milk shake. Much smaller margin snails are sometimes seen feeding on the same fish. These also suck out the body juices of parrotfish and other sound sleepers, but they climb on the fish's body and insert their much shorter proboscises between the

A vampire snail crawls on the nearly invisible mucus cocoon of a sleeping parrotfish—visible only due to the grains of sand scattered on it—and extends its feeding proboscis into the mouth of the parrotfish. A second snail, below the fish's chin, prepares to attack as well.

The colorful, but thin, shell of this porcelain crab provides support for its body and some defense against predators and parasites. But it cannot protect the crab from "body-snatching" parasitic barnacles that attach to the outside of the shell, puncture it, and inject cells inside to take over the crab's body.

scales to pierce the skin. Sometimes dozens of margin snails can be found attacking the same fish.

INVASION OF THE BODY SNATCHERS.

The ingenious crab-castrating barnacle is but one example of a parasite that takes control of its host's body, like an alien in a science fiction film, and uses it for its own purposes. This organism has a free-swimming larval stage virtually identical to that of any other barnacle. When it finds a suitable host, though, it cements itself to the crab's body and metamorphoses into something quite different. This, however, is but a short-lived stage, which exists only to puncture the crab's shell and inject into it the internal stage of the parasite. The internal stage begins as a small mass, which develops rapidly into a rootlike network that infiltrates the crab, absorbing its vital fluids to nourish the barnacle's own growth. The barnacle also takes control of the crab's nervous system, altering its hormone production. It may inhibit the crab from molting, a process by which crabs both grow and rid themselves of parasites. The crab will not need to grow, since the nutrients it gets from food are now supporting the growth of the parasite instead. If it is a male crab, it is castrated and begins to develop female characteristics.

The parasite is now ready to reproduce. It punctures the crab's abdomen again and develops a reproductive organ on the underside of the crab exactly where the crab's own egg mass would be if it were allowed to reproduce. As the barnacle's eggs develop—around 200,000 in a clutch—the crab cares for them as it would its own. It carefully fans and grooms the reproductive organ, even while it continues to clean itself of other parasites that attach to it. The crab has become a docile zombie in the service of the parasitic barnacle. When the eggs are ready to hatch, the crab lifts itself up, waves its abdomen, and fans the reproductive organ to create a current, into which the barnacle releases its larvae to be dispersed and search for new crabs to attack.

The barnacle allows the crab just enough of its own resources to stay alive and continue feeding so that it can support the barnacle's continued reproduction. During a three-month breeding season, the barnacle can produce more than a million eggs. As with fish lice, only the female of the species attacks the crab. The male barnacle instead parasitizes the female of its own species. It enters her as a larva and lives within her, serving only to produce sperm to fertilize her eggs. The female barnacle thus never has to look for a mate. The barnacle's life is not as easy as

it might seem, though. It may be attacked by other types of parasitic crustaceans, in addition to having to support the male of its own species. Parasites upon other parasites are common enough to have earned their own name: hyperparasites.

DAVID AND GOLIATH. Even the most ferocious sharks fall victim to small parasites against which they are defenseless. Mako sharks, possibly the fastest and most ravenous fish in the ocean, cannot escape the simple crustaceans known

Even the mako shark, considered one of the most ferocious animals in the sea, falls victim to parasites. This mako has stringlike parasitic copepods (a type of crustacean) trailing from its dorsal fin.

An elephant seal resting on the beach reveals a bloody wound caused by the attack of a cookie-cutter shark. The shark attaches to its victim's body, creates a suction with its mouth, and twists its body around until it has cut out a scoop of flesh.

as copepods. They attach themselves to the sharks' dorsal fins, decorating the rear edge like streamers. The sharks' mouths often bristle with clusters of parasites attached to the roof or floor of the mouth. Other parasites garnish the flanks and the underside of the head of many sharks or cling to the gill slits. Sometimes copepods can be seen even attached to the claspers, or sex organs, of male sharks.

Some sharks are themselves predatory parasites. The cookie-cutter shark, which feeds on whales, dolphins, and large fish, does not attach permanently to a host, but it qualifies as a parasite because it does not kill its prey. This diminutive fish, less than two feet long, attacks even giant whales, lurking in the depths until its prey approaches, then lunging forward to sink its jaws into the victim's flesh.

The lower jaw is shaped like an ice cream scoop with sharp, serrated edges. The shark creates a powerful suction with its jaws as it twists its body around, removing a spherical plug of flesh from the victim. The question is, how does the cookie-cutter lure its prey into attack range?

These sharks have luminous tissue within their mouths. Scientists speculate that they may wait in the darkness of the midocean depths with their mouths open and the lining glowing. They could resemble the luminous squid, which are a major food source for many of the larger marine animals. When such an animal

Although small, the cookie-cutter shark attacks prey many times larger than itself. Probably it attracts its victims by revealing luminous tissue in its mouth, which glows like small shrimp or squid in the darkness of the deep ocean. (Photo shows a preserved specimen.)

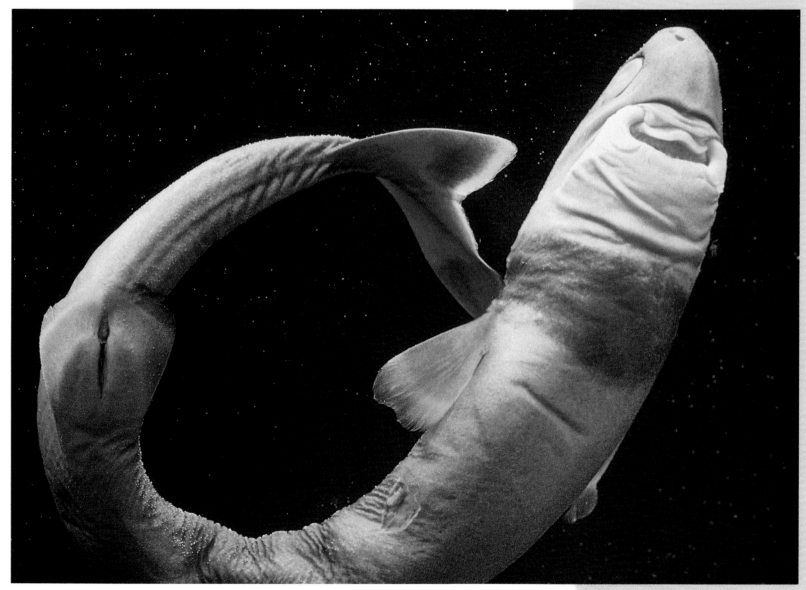

Below: *A carp is parasitized by lampreys. Various types of lampreys occur in both fresh and saltwater and attack prey from medium-sized fish up to great whales.* Opposite: *Lampreys cause millions of dollars of losses annually to the fishing industry in the Great Lakes. The only effective control method found is poisoning the shallow areas where the larvae occur.*

approaches to investigate, instead of a meal, it gets a very unpleasant surprise. On very dark nights, cookie-cutter sharks may migrate upward to the surface of the ocean. There are even cases in which they have fed on humans. It is believed, however, that the victims had drowned prior to the attack.

Sea lampreys are primitive jawless fish that attack larger fish and whales much as the cookie-cutter shark does. But unlike the shark, once a sea lamprey has attached to its victim, it doesn't let go. It continues to rasp away the victim's flesh and suck body fluids through the jawless oral disc until the victim dies. After the Great Lakes were artificially connected to the ocean by the St. Lawrence

4
2

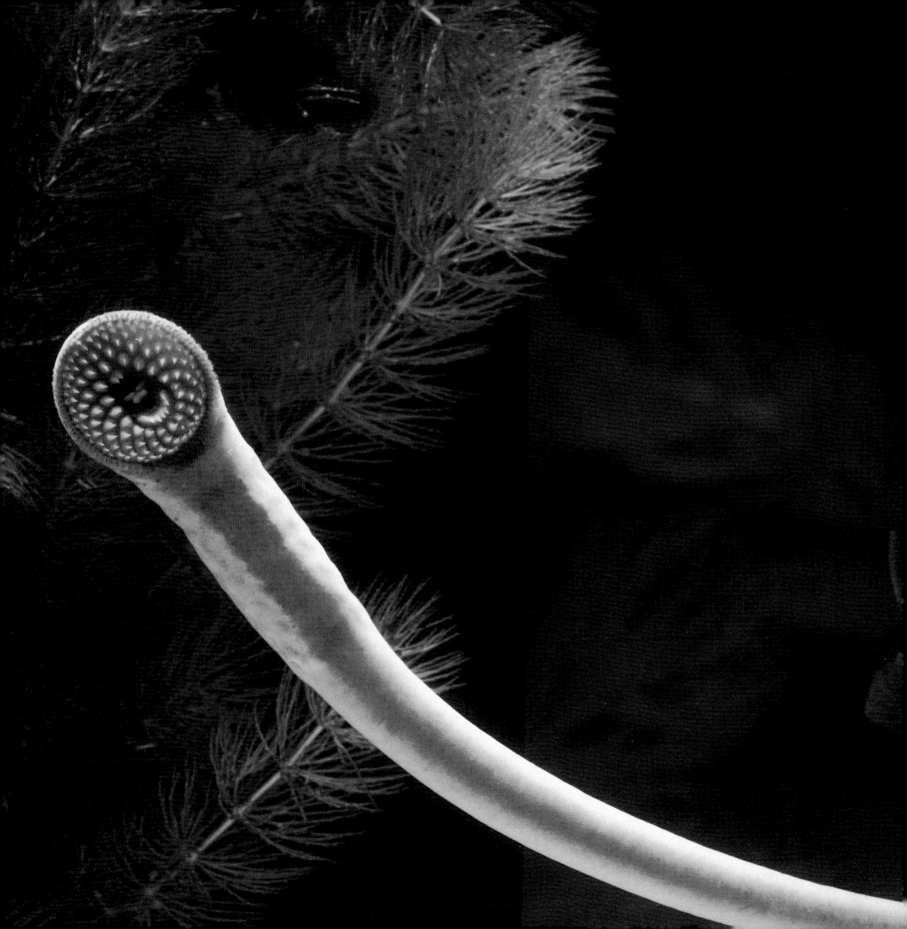

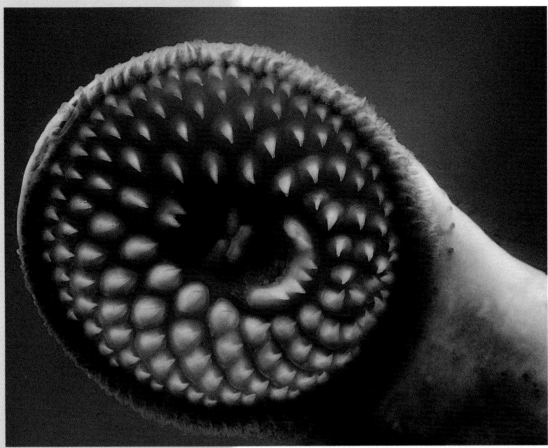

The oral disc of a lamprey is covered with small teeth that rasp away at the flesh of its victim. The lamprey has no jaws. It attaches its disc by suction while it consumes the flesh and body fluids of its prey.

Seaway, lampreys invaded the lakes and nearly wiped out the fisheries they supported. Years and millions of dollars later, the lampreys are kept under control by annual applications of poison. Some of the great whales, especially sei whales, frequently have their bodies covered with oval scars, which could have been caused by lampreys, by cookie-cutter sharks, or by parasitic worms.

PARASITIC HORDES. Whales are also victimized by smaller parasites called amphipods, a type of crustacean related to copepods. Known as whale lice, these fingernail-size crablike creatures live in skin folds of the great whales. They achieve large numbers in the slower-moving whales, such as gray whales and right whales. More than 100,000 of one species of whale lice were removed from a single gray whale. On these whales they are found in such concentrations that they appear as solid yellowish-white masses, especially around barnacles, which also attach to the skin of gray whales, and on callosities on right whales.

Callosities—raised areas of hardened skin—are a unique feature of right whales. The callosity sites are already formed at birth and harden as the animal grows. Why these whales should develop such cancerous-looking growths is an unsolved mystery. One theory is that they provide sites to concentrate the populations of whale lice. Another is that males use the rough patches as horns when competing for access to females. Males have slightly larger callosities than females, which gives some credence to this theory. Whatever their purpose, the callosities provide a fertile area for the growth of whale lice, which feed mainly upon the skin of the whale, and also for barnacles.

Barnacles, also a type of crustacean, use their comblike legs to filter plankton from the water. They rely on their host only for a site of attachment and transportation. They can attach to many parts of a whale's body and are frequently seen on the snout, the flippers, and the underside. Female humpback

Throat pleats of a humpback whale bulge out as it surfaces after swallowing a huge volume of herring and seawater. Note the cluster of tan-colored barnacles on one side of the throat and the white ring scars left where other barnacle have detached.

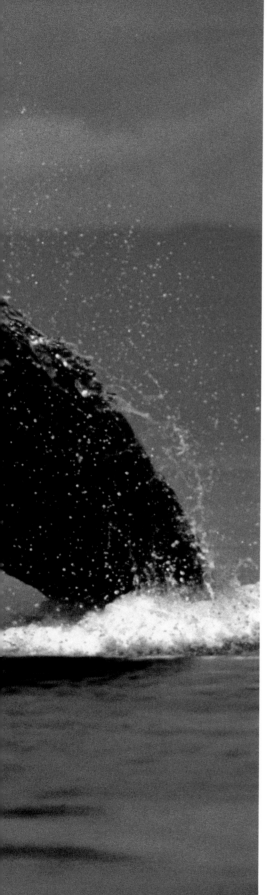

whales often carry thick growths of barnacles, with sharp-edged shells, around their mammary slits and genital organs. This does not seem to discourage males from mating with them, but how they do so without extreme discomfort or injury is hard to imagine. The offspring of these whales of course have no choice but to nurse from them. The babies have sometimes been seen with injuries apparently caused during nursing by the barnacle shells.

BREACHING. The reasons why whales breach, or leap out of the water, may never be fully known. They may do so for different reasons at different times. One purpose that has been proposed is to dislodge parasites such as barnacles and whale lice. Basking sharks, which can grow to a length of 30 to 40 feet—as large as a whale—have also been seen breaching out of the water on occasion, and the same explanation is suggested. Basking sharks are subject to a variety of different parasites, including lampreys, and this may be their only way of getting rid of them. Sperm whales appear to have very few external parasites. This may be because they dive to great depths, believed to exceed 9,000 feet. External parasites may not be able to survive the water pressure at this depth, which exceeds 4,000

Opposite: *A humpback whale breaches in a mighty display of power. One function of these displays may be to dislodge parasites and commensals, such as the tan-colored barnacles visible on the throat, flank, genital region, and pectoral fins.*

pounds per square inch. Young sperm whales, which cannot dive that deep, are frequently covered with remoras, but adults are not seen with them.

TRANSFORMATION. "Fish lice" are isopods, yet another type of related crustacean. Though usually reaching a size of only an inch or less, they are often quite large in comparison to the size of their hosts. A soldierfish with an isopod attached to the forehead, common in many parts of the Caribbean, appears to be wearing a grotesque oversize bonnet. Fish lice sink their claws into the body of their host and feed directly on the body juices. Curiously, different species of fishes, or the same fish in different areas, have different patterns of parasite attachment. Some may have one isopod in the center of the forehead, while others have one on each cheek. It is very rare to see more than two fish lice on a reef fish.

Why the fish do nothing to rid themselves of these grotesque, alien attachments, such as bashing them against a coral head, is an enigma. The answer may lie in the sex life of the isopods. Although the fish may appear

The position where a parasitic isopod attaches to its host is consistent for a certain species of fish in a certain location. In the Cayman Islands, many of the black-bar soldierfish have an isopod—only one, always attached to the center of the forehead.

to have only one or two isopods, there are actually many more. The large ones are females, while many smaller males live inconspicuously on the fish's skin, feeding harmlessly on scales and mucus. The female exudes a chemical that prevents any of the males from changing sex. If the female is removed or killed, one of the males becomes a female, grows rapidly to a larger size, and adopts a parasitic lifestyle.

One type of isopod parasite attaches to the tongue of the fish and feeds on this organ. As the tongue is consumed, the parasite grows larger, replacing the

The parasitic isopod attached to the cheek of this grouper is related to the terrestrial isopods known as pill bugs or sow bugs, commonly found in gardens. The parasite is a female. The males are much smaller and feed only on bits of skin and mucus.

lost portion. Eventually the entire tongue is eaten and the isopod itself replaces its function, allowing the fish to continue to feed. A good parasite never kills its host, since it might well kill itself by doing so.

Sushi Alert

Parasites are most easily seen when they attach to the external surface of an organism, but internal parasites are common as well. Some of these parasites have extremely complex life cycles, which may involve a variety of different hosts, sometimes including both terrestrial and marine animals. Salmon, for example, may be infested with a type of worm that passes from bird to freshwater snail to marine fish to grizzly bear during the course of its elaborate life cycle. It thus traverses most of the major habitat types on Earth in the course of just one generation. This, and other parasites that normally infect mammals, can also pose a threat to humans, since our physiology is similar enough to that of the normal host to allow the parasite to survive. Therefore, eating raw salmon—or fish with similar life histories—is particularly hazardous for us. Fish parasites are killed by cooking or, in most cases, by freezing.

PARASITES ASSIST BIOLOGISTS. The stage of a parasite when it can infect a host may have very specific requirements that point to a small geographic area and/or a particular season. Parasites of this type can be useful to marine biologists in their research. If a certain species of parasite is found in a fish, biologists can infer that this fish passed through a certain area at a certain time, when that parasite was in its infective stage. This technique has been used successfully to study the migration patterns of salmon in southern Australia, using the cysts of tapeworms found in the gut. Salmon are intermediate hosts for this type of tapeworm. The eggs hatch in seawater into tiny larvae, some of which are eaten by filter-feeding planktonic copepods. The infected copepods are eaten by small fish, such as anchovies, which are eaten by larger fish, including salmon. Sharks, which eat the larger fish, are believed to be the "definitive hosts," which house the final stage of the worms that releases the eggs. In this way, parasites can act as natural markers or biological tags to identify fish, or other animals, from a certain area. Natural markers can replace the metal and plastic tags that biologists often use to mark fish.

SKINHEADS AND SKIN THIEVES. Kleptoparasites make their living by stealing food collected by another organism. The classic example is frigate birds—large, powerful seabirds capable of skimming their own fish from the sea surface, but who do not dive and prefer to steal their fish from other birds. Their usual victims are boobies, deep-diving birds that are excellent fishers. A frigate will

A male (with red throat) and female frigate bird soar effortlessly on wide, powerful wings. Excellent flyers, they are capable of catching their own fish when it is close to the surface, but normally they prefer to steal from other birds.

pursue a booby relentlessly, tugging and pecking at it until it drops or regurgitates its fish, and then will catch the food in midair as it falls.

Some dolphins and small whales may occasionally engage in kleptoparasitism. Pilot whales, spotted dolphins, and bottlenose dolphins have all been observed harassing sperm whales—circling them, jumping around them, and in some cases thrashing the whales with their flukes. The whales often react to such provocations by diving to escape or by gathering into defensive formations. In at least one case, they regurgitated squid. It may be that the dolphins and pilot whales (actually large dolphins) were just having fun or being mischievous, but it may be that they were deliberately trying to make the sperm whales regurgitate

Dolphins are highly social animals, usually seen traveling in groups, like this pod of Atlantic spotted dolphins.

their squid in order to feed on it. Or the relationship may be more complex than we have yet been able to discern.

Many kinds of dolphins also bow-ride on various types of whales, getting a free ride by coasting on the pressure wave pushed ahead of the whale as it swims. It is not known whether they do this for fun, to save energy while traveling, or both, but they often seem to go out of their way to catch up to a whale. The whales sometimes seem annoyed by this and occasionally lunge at the dolphins. Right whales in Argentina are also harassed by kelp gulls, which land on their backs and peck off bits of skin and blubber, a straightforward case of parasitism. The attack often causes the whale to flinch and swim away. Repeated attacks may force whales to abandon favored areas for resting and nursing their calves, which may adversely affect the recovery of the population from whaling.

THE SILVER LINING. Biologists recognize that classification of symbiotic relationships into categories of mutualism, parasitism, and so forth, is somewhat arbitrary. In reality, a fine gradation of relationships exists in nature, with each category blending subtly into the others. Some biologists prefer to think of all types of symbiosis as just different kinds of parasitism. And even the most harmful kinds of parasitism may produce great benefits through evolution. The complex cell structure of higher animals may have resulted from ancient parasitism of unicellular microbes upon other single-celled creatures. And some scientists believe that the evolution of sex enabled host organisms to swap genes in order to increase resistance to parasitic infections.

A Southern right whale's callosities are sites for whale lice.

New Generations

Some female fish lice control the sex of their dwarf male subordinates through chemical mastery. If the female is killed, the chemical she exudes is removed and one of the males becomes a female to take her place. This may sound like science fiction to us, but such a system is not at all unusual in the ocean, where reproductive methods include almost every possible scenario by which an organism can make a copy of itself. Changing sex in midlife is

55

Normally spaced out in individual territories, Nassau groupers can blanket the reef when they get together for their annual spawning aggregation. When this picture was taken, tens of thousands of fish carpeted the reef.

the rule, rather than the exception, in many groups of organisms. Most groupers, or sea basses, for example, mature first as females. Some of the females later change to males. Large males are much more successful at spawning than small ones, so it seems to make sense to be a female while you're small.

WILD PARTY. Nassau groupers are normally solitary, territorial fish, driving other members of their species away when they encounter them. Their loner lifestyle makes reproduction a problem. They solve this by having mass gatherings under the full moon once a year, usually very close to the beginning of the

The Nassau grouper at the center retains most of the normal barred color pattern, while the one just behind it has changed into the bicolor (black above, white below) spawning pattern.

year. Groupers travel for many miles to special meeting places where they gather in aggregations of up to thousands of fish, all looking for mates.

During most of the year, the Nassau grouper has a fairly fixed color pattern of diagonal bars. It may blanch a little bit under certain circumstances, but it is not a chameleon of the reef. The rules change when it arrives at the big New Year's party. At least a half dozen different color patterns are exhibited as the fish interact with other members of their species. Scientists are baffled by what meanings most of these might have for the fish. The significance of one pattern, though, is very clear. When most of the fish have changed from bars to a bicolor phase—black on top and white on the bottom, with a white diagonal stripe through the eye—they are ready to spawn.

As nightfall begins to cloak the reef in darkness, the aggregation breaks up into smaller groups of females surrounded by males. Suddenly a female, followed by her entourage, shoots up from the reef toward the surface of the ocean. At the peak of her dash, she sheds her eggs into the water. The males spray milt around the eggs, looking like jet fighters leaving white vapor trails behind them as they soar through the darkening water. The fertilized eggs are carried offshore by the outgoing tide, where they will join the plankton community in the open sea. The

As night falls, Nassau groupers in a spawning aggregation begin to change to their spawning colors. The fish at bottom center is in full spawning colors with a black back, white belly, and diagonal white stripe through the eye.

57

Opposite: Nudibranchs (sea slugs with exposed gills) mating. During mating, a nudibranch often both passes sperm to its partner and receives sperm from the partner, playing both the male and female roles at the same time.

length of a fish's larval life may depend upon how long it takes for currents to bring it back into shallow water. After a month or more, the larvae descend to the reef and metamorphose into tiny Nassau groupers—all females.

PLAYING TWO ROLES.

Another group of sea basses—the small reef fish known as hamlets—do not change sex as they mature. Instead, they are both male and female at the same time. A hamlet can mate with any member of its species. It does not have to search for the opposite sex, since all hamlets are both. When spawning begins, one hamlet assumes the role of a male and the other a female. They circle each other with the female releasing eggs and the male releasing milt. After a few moments, the roles are reversed, with the former female fertilizing the eggs of the former male. Hamlets will apparently mate with any other hamlet they meet at the right time. The related harlequin bass are monogamous. They mate with the same partner every day, but each gets to be both the husband and the wife.

The situation is even more complicated with some of the other small basses. Tobaccofish are hermaphrodites (they have both male and female reproductive organs). But as they grow larger, they tend to mate more often as males than females and may break off a spawning bout without giving their partner a chance to play the male. Lantern basses start life as hermaphrodites but may switch to pure male behavior when they get older. The males keep harems of hermaphrodites, which usually spawn as females but occasionally as males.

Nudibranchs—sea slugs that are often brightly colored—take hermaphroditism one

Social Identity Control

Anemonefish, like groupers, are sequential hermaphrodites—they get to be both male and female, but not at the same time. However, unlike groupers, they make their switch from male to female. In most species only one pair of anemonefish on an anemone is reproductive. The largest fish is the female, and the next largest is the male. If something happens to the female, the male reverses sex. It takes a few weeks for the testes to change into ovaries and begin to produce eggs. However, the fish begins to exhibit female behaviors within hours. This indicates that the fish's sexual identity is decided by its brain, even though the process is almost certainly not conscious. Since the fish makes its "decision" based upon the status of the other fish in the group, scientists refer to this process as social sex determination. When the male switches to female, the largest juvenile then matures rapidly to become a functional male.

A nudibranch deposits its eggs on the reef in a delicate whorled ribbon. After completing the roselike arrangement, the slug will crawl off and leave the eggs to develop and hatch on their own. The larvae, unlike the adults, have shells.

step further. When they couple, they mate as both females and males at the same instant. Each slug inserts its male organ into the female organ of the other so it can fertilize its partner's eggs and have its own eggs fertilized simultaneously.

MALE AND SUPERMALE. Wrasses and parrotfish have separate sexes and start life as either male or female. However, things are not as clear-cut as that might imply. Whereas some of the ladies retain their femininity, others metamorphose into supermales—large individuals with distinctive color patterns that play a dominant role in reproduction. In some species, males also can become super-males, but in other species this privilege is reserved for females that reverse sex.

Males of some species of wrasses intensify their colors during courtship to really impress the females. In other types of fish, the male, female, or both may completely change their color pattern during courtship. Both may adopt the same spawning colors, or they may adopt completely different patterns. In jacks, for instance, one partner remains silver, and the other turns black. When a pair of white-spotted filefish match up, one partner exhibits white spots while the other displays an orange saddle.

The supermale, or terminal phase, of the stoplight parrotfish is blue and green, with a bright yellow spot on the gill cover. Females and initial-phase males are completely different in appearance, with a mottled dark and light pattern on the back and a red belly and tail.

Above: *The color pattern of the rainbow wrasse supermale is so different from that of the initial-phase fish that it appears to be a different species. The supermales are able to pair-spawn with a large number of females in succession.* Opposite: *Group spawning by initial-phase rainbow wrasses. The fish rush upward in a cluster and release eggs and sperm into the water.*

Among the bluehead wrasses (named for the color pattern of the supermales), only the supermales hold spawning territories and pair-spawn with females. The smaller males, which exhibit the same plain yellow color pattern as the females, are also able to spawn, but only in groups. Spawning occurs at specific times of day—around noon in the best-studied population. Clouds of dozens to hundreds of small male wrasses gather together on the reef with one to a few females. They all rush upward in a mass, releasing eggs and milt together in a white cloud.

The supermales, which can pair-spawn successively with large numbers of females, have a better chance of parenthood. They don't have the sperm of other

The supermale bluehead wrasses dominate the spawning territories, enabling them to breed more success-fully than the initial-phase males, which are smaller and yellow, like the females. The initial-phase males, lacking territories, typically group-spawn with other initial males and a smaller number of females.

males competing to fertilize the eggs. Not all of the subordinate males play by the rules, however. Some of them, referred to as streakers, improve their odds by waiting until a supermale has enticed a female to release eggs in his territory. They then dash in, discharge some milt, and flee before they can be punished. When parrotfish reverse sex (from female to male), they begin to produce sperm before they complete their color change. During this period they are particularly effective as streakers, because they are males that look like females.

PLASTIC IDENTITY. Bluehead wrasses may change their gender later in life, but at least they start out as either male or female. One might imagine from this that sex is determined genetically, as it is in humans. This does not, however, appear to be the case. The sex ratio of blueheads varies from one reef to another and is mathematically related to the size of the reef. The reef's size controls the number of mating territories available, which determines the optimum ratio of males to females for the greatest reproductive potential on that reef. The actual ratio is very close to the optimal, meaning that somehow, the larval fish "choose" to be male or female based at least partly on the characteristics of the reef where they settle. This implies that a larval wrasse carried to a reef by the currents would be able to assess not only the reef's size but also the sex of all the wrasses on that reef. How this could be accomplished is a mystery.

In some species of wrasses, whether or not a female reverses sex is controlled solely by the sex ratio of the population. In still others it is controlled by the size ratio—how many fish are bigger than that individual, and how many are smaller, without regard to sex. Generally, among wrasses and the related parrotfishes, there are several females for every male.

The sex of the individual at conception is also indeterminate, or plastic, in a number of other organisms. Sex is determined by the environment in many reptiles,

Gender Chaos

A nondescript four-inch basslet found in the eastern Pacific known as the banded serrano has one of the most complex and variable mating systems of any marine fish yet studied. Serranos mature first as simultaneous hermaphrodites, with both male and female sex organs. If population density is low, they form monogamous pairs. During the reproductive season, the pairs spawn every afternoon, with the larger fish acting first as a male, then as a female.

If the population density is higher, the dominant fish organize harems. Dominant hermaphrodites pair-spawn as males with all of the fish in their harems. The subordinate fish normally spawn only as females, and only with the dominant fish. However, some of them may take the male role as streakers during a spawn between the dominant fish and another subordinate, and later take the female role when they spawn with the dominant fish. The dominant fish, after spawning as males with their own harem, may go outside their territory and spawn as females with the dominant fish of a nearby harem. The largest fish lose their female organs and become pure males. Dominant fish can be either male or hermaphroditic.

In very dense populations, subharems form within the harems. The dominant fish, a male, spawns

Banded serrano

with the subdominant fish, which are hermaphrodites. After spawning as females with the dominant fish, the subdominants then spawn as males with the subordinate fish in their subharems. The smaller fish usually spawn only as females, but some release male gametes by streaking.

An olive ridley turtle digs a nest on the beach. Ridley turtles nest in "arribadas," which is a Spanish word referring to arrival in harbor. An arribada can consist of thousands of turtles coming ashore at once to lay their eggs on the same stretch of beach.

including sea turtles. In this case, the deciding factor is the temperature of the sand the eggs are incubated in. Female sea turtles leave the ocean to lay their eggs on sandy beaches. The depth of the nest, the characteristics of the sand itself, and the weather all affect the temperature of the sand. At a certain temperature, half the eggs will hatch as male turtles and the other half as females. If the temperature is higher, more will hatch as females. At lower temperatures, more

eggs become male, reaching 100 percent if the temperature is low enough. A temperature difference of only 4½ degrees Fahrenheit can make the difference between a nest that is all female and one that is all male. Attempts to boost turtle populations by removing nests to hatcheries may backfire if the shaded hatcheries are rearing turtles that are all male. Beach renourishment projects also may be affecting the reproductive capacity of sea turtles. The sand used is often

Above: *A female leatherback sea turtle deposits her eggs in a pit she has dug in a sandy beach in the tropics. After laying several nests, she will leave the eggs to incubate on their own, and she will swim thousands of miles back to higher latitudes to feed on sea jellies.* Left: *Green sea turtles emerge from the nest and crawl toward the ocean. How many of these are male and how many are female depends upon the temperature in the nest during the incubation of the eggs.*

Above: *A hatchling green sea turtle makes its way from the nest on a sandy beach into the sea.* Opposite: *A pair of mating green sea turtles swims toward the surface to take a breath of air. The female does all the swimming for the couple. The male, on top, merely hangs on and curls his long tail around underneath the female's shell.*

imported and may have different composition and grain size from the natural sand, resulting in a higher or lower temperature at nest depth.

MALES—WHO NEEDS THEM? Sea turtles have internal fertilization. The eggs are fertilized inside the body of the female. However, this does not occur during mating. The sperm is stored separately from the eggs. It may be used to fertilize several batches of eggs over a period of months. If a female turtle mates once at the beginning of the egg-laying season, she may not need a male again until the following year. Perhaps realizing it may be their last chance, male turtles

A female green sea turtle carries two suitors, one on top of the other. The males hold on so tightly that fishermen can capture the whole group by tying a line to the flipper of one turtle.

are very persistent. The male turtle mounts on top of the female and grips her shell with the claws on his flippers. If the female resists, the male bites her on the back of the neck to subdue her. The female must then pull the male as she swims and lift him above the water in order to breathe. It may be hours before he releases her.

Sometimes one or more additional males will mount the male that is holding the female, increasing her load and nearly drowning her. South Sea islanders sometimes capture two or more turtles at once by swimming up to a mating group and tying a rope around the female's flipper. The males will not release their grip, even as they are hauled back to the canoe. On other islands, fishermen make decoys resembling turtles and tow them through the water during mating season. When a male turtle mounts the decoy, they haul it back to the boat.

Most fish and invertebrates (animals without backbones) reproduce by spawning. Eggs and sperm are simultaneously cast into the sea, where they hope to find each other. Even in those invertebrates that mate, fertilization is usually external. The sperm are stored in, or on, the body of the female until her eggs are mature. The sperm are later taken from storage and used to fertilize the eggs as they are passed out of the body. In spiny lobsters, the sperm are deposited on the underside of the female in a hard, black patch known to divers as a tar spot. By turning a female over and looking for the tar spot, a

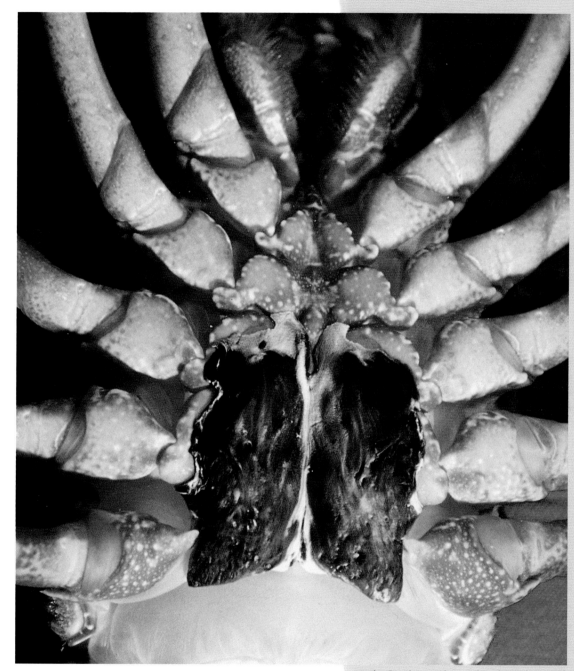

The dark patch on this female spiny lobster is a spermatophore deposited by a male. When the female extrudes her eggs onto her abdomen, she will scratch open the spermatophore to release the sperm.

A female spiny lobster carries a mass of orange eggs on the underside of her tail. When the eggs hatch, she will fan the larvae out into the current, where they will enter the drifting phase of their life cycle.

fisherman can tell if she has mated or not. On some crabs the sperm may remain viable for as long as a year, and it can be used to fertilize multiple batches of eggs. During this time, the female can produce millions of off-spring without having any contact with a male.

Other creatures dispense with males altogether. Some species of brine shrimp and ostracods (tiny clamlike crustaceans) consist entirely of fe-males. This anomaly also occurs in some types of fresh and brackish-water fishes, lizards, geckos, and insects. These Amazon races reproduce by cloning exact copies of the mother. Although some types of single-sex animals mate with males of closely related species, these males do not fertilize the eggs.

FINDING A MATE WHILE STUCK TO THE SEAFLOOR.

Many invertebrates spend part or all of their lives attached to the bottom of the sea. This poses some difficulties when it comes to finding a mate. Most of these animals have solved the problem by letting seawater act as the go-between. Chemical cues tell each animal when its neigh-bors are spawning, and it releases its gametes into the ocean at the same time, sending them off to a rendezvous with the gametes of unknown partners.

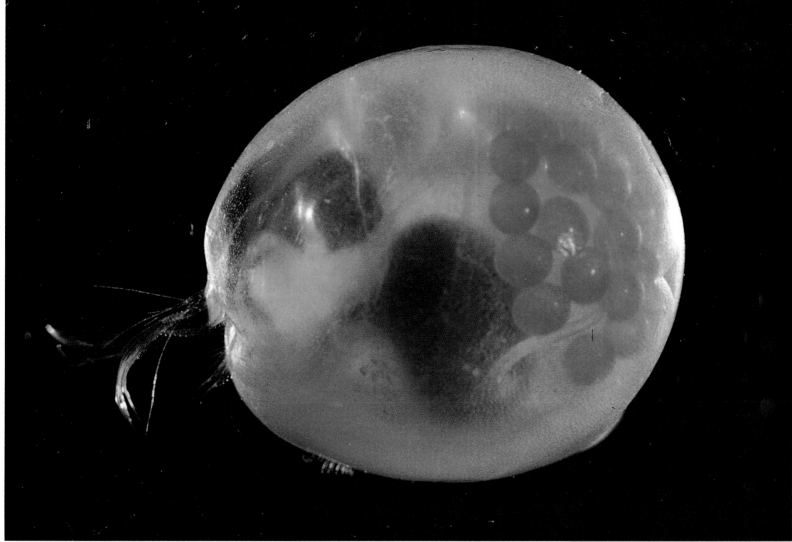

Some ostracods are tiny crustaceans with two-part shells that make them look more like a clam than a crustacean. This deepwater ostracod is a female with eggs that can be seen through the transparent shell. Some species of ostracods consist entirely of females, which reproduce by cloning themselves.

Barnacles, however, have chosen to stick with the old-fashioned way of doing things. Even though barnacles may cluster together, each lives alone in its own shell, which it never leaves. But barnacles have evolved a way to mate without moving. The muscular penis of the barnacle can extend to five times its resting length, greatly exceeding the length of the animal's body. Relative to body size, it is the longest penis in the animal kingdom. This allows it to reach out of the owner's shell and into the home of a neighbor. Still, not very many neighbors are within reach. What if all the neighbors happened to be male? Most barnacles are hermaphrodites, assuring that any member of the species within reach will be

Undersea Beehives

In at least one species of marine shrimp, most individuals do not reproduce at all. Recently discovered colonies of sponge-dwelling snapping shrimp in the Caribbean would resemble convents were it not for the queen. She does all of the egg-laying for the colony, which can number more than 300 members. Since most of them are the queen's offspring, the worker shrimps may actually help to propagate their own genes when they help to take care of her eggs. The larvae that hatch will be the brothers and sisters of the workers that care for them—potentially sharing at least 50 percent of their genetic code.

This type of social system has also been found in bees, ants, termites, and African mole rats. The sponges the shrimps live in resemble, at least superficially, termite mounds or beehives. Some scientists speculate that the habit of nesting in cavities of these sorts, by maintaining relatives in close proximity, promotes development of complex social systems with castes, cooperative brood care, and division of labor.

Opposite: Sharks reproduce by mating, with internal fertilization, as do mammals. The claspers, or sex organs, of this male great white shark can be seen toward the rear of its body, behind the pectoral fin.

the correct gender. As an exception to the rule, some barnacles are female but keep a dwarf male with them to fertilize their eggs.

DANGEROUS LIAISONS.

Fish belonging to one large and unusual group mate and have internal fertilization, like turtles and marine mammals. Unlike turtles, many members of this group give live birth. These are the sharks and rays. The male shark has two sex organs, known as claspers, which are analogous to the penis of a mammal and are used to funnel semen into the female. Unlike a male crab, which inserts both its sex organs into the two receptacles of the female at the same time, the shark can insert only one clasper at a time into the single opening of the female. To accomplish this delicate maneuver while swimming in the ocean, the male shark must grasp the female. But the shark has no hands. So it uses the only tool at its disposal—its teeth.

The clasper of a sand tiger shark protrudes behind its pelvic fin. Male sharks have two of these sex organs, but only insert one at a time into the female during mating.

The presence of "mating scars" makes a useful tool for biologists to determine if a female shark has recently mated. In some species, females have skin almost twice as thick as that of the males—a trait with obvious survival value for the females. Even though some females receive serious gashes over large portions of their bodies during mating season, survival seems to be high, and the scars tend to heal rapidly.

Gestation is normally slightly less than a year, but it is nearly two years in some species. During this time, in the live-bearing species, the embryos are nour-

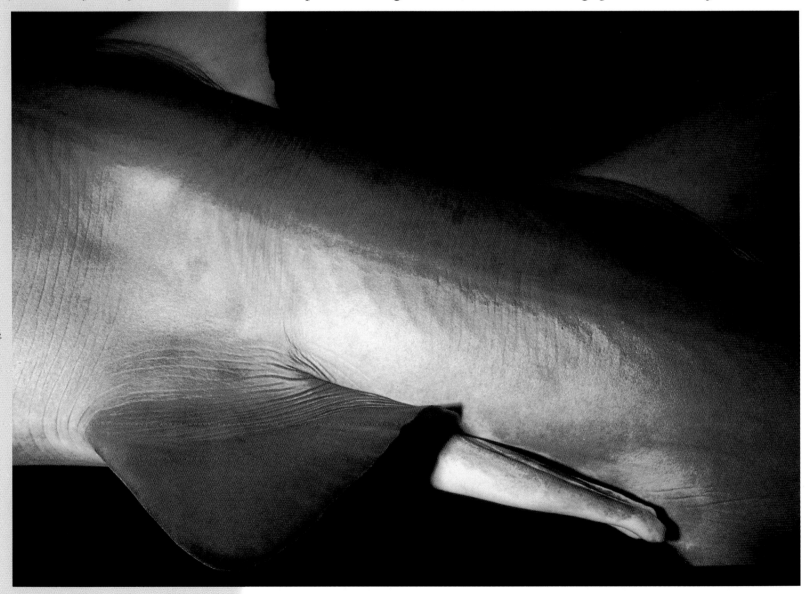

ished by a pseudo placenta that is remarkably similar to a human placenta—and which evolved millions of years earlier. Not all sharks give live birth, however. Some sharks deposit the fertilized egg on the seafloor and leave the embryo to develop at the mercy of the sea.

ROLE REVERSAL. Many marine organisms give no care at all to their eggs and merely cast them adrift in the ocean currents to fend for themselves. They count on sheer numbers to compensate for the eggs' poor odds of survival. Some produce millions of eggs each year. An oyster can spawn 200 million eggs in a year; a cod, 90 million. Those fish that provide some care for their eggs produce a smaller number.

Contrary to the general rule in the rest of the animal kingdom, it is often the male that cares for the eggs. Male damselfishes usually prepare a nest into which the female lays her eggs. After fertilizing the eggs, the father maintains a

Above: A male sergeant major damselfish carries a sea star away from its egg patch. The male will guard its nest continuously, day and night, chasing off any intruder that might be a threat to the eggs, until they hatch. This leaves the father very few opportunities for feeding. Left: A male sergeant major damselfish tends its patch of red eggs. The female's responsibility ended when she laid her eggs in this male's territory, leaving them for him to fertilize and protect until hatching.

vigilant guard over them, chasing off any potential predators, fanning the eggs to aerate them, and grooming them with his mouth. Some damselfishes, such as the sergeant major, change color when they are guarding a nest.

Male jawfish take egg custody a step further, incubating the eggs in their mouths. Every so often the jawfish spits out the egg mass and rolls it around to aerate it before taking it back into his mouth. Reversal of sex roles reaches its extreme, however, in sea horses and sea dragons. In these fish, the female deposits her eggs into a brood pouch on the male's abdomen, where he fertilizes

Opposite: *After fertilizing the eggs laid by his partner, the male jawfish takes them into his mouth for brooding. Here they will be both protected from predators and carefully tended.* Below: *A male yellow-headed jawfish broods a cluster of eggs in its mouth.*

them. The eggs implant in the soft membrane lining the pouch. Oxygen and nutrients are passed through the membrane to the developing embryos. As they grow, the male becomes visibly pregnant, with a swollen belly. When the baby sea horses are fully developed, he expels them with violent contractions, and even seems to un-

7
9

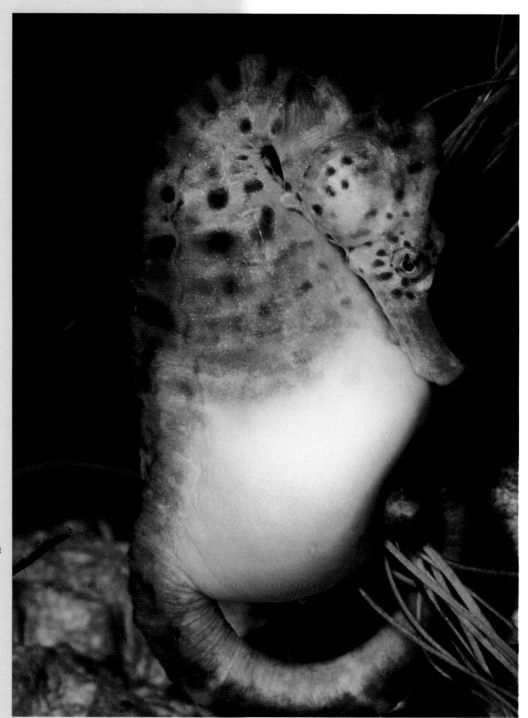

The belly of a "pregnant" male sea horse is swollen with the eggs developing inside its brood pouch.

dergo labor pains. Over a period of days, a sea horse can give birth to up to 1,000 babies.

What remains unexplained is how these male marine fishes wound up with this chore. A tidy and widely accepted explanation accounts for child-rearing usually falling to the female of the species. An egg contains quite a bit of protein, carbohydrates, and other metabolically "expensive" substances that the female has to produce. Her energy investment in each egg is high. A sperm cell contains only a bit of genetic coding with a tail. Sperm is "cheap." The female, with the greater investment in the bargain, should have a greater incentive to spend additional energy caring for the fertilized egg. The male should get a better return on his investment by spreading his cheap sperm around as widely as possible. It seems to work that way nearly everywhere except in a few quirky fish. The reason why these fish should be any different remains a mystery.

CANNIBAL DADS AND CANNIBAL BRIDES. Some of the doting fathers, though, are not quite the superparents they appear to be at first glance. The male garibaldi, a large striking orange damselfish found in California, prepares a nest and entices females to lay eggs in it. He carefully fans and grooms the eggs, like any other damselfish. But from time to time, just as the eggs are getting ready to hatch, he eats a batch of them. How could such a behavior evolve, researchers wondered? The driving force behind evolution is the need for each organism to pass its genes on to future generations. Sometimes the health or even the life of the parent is sacrificed in the act of reproduction. A seemingly selfish act such as eating the offspring doesn't seem to make biological sense.

Hours of underwater observation, however, provided an answer. A garibaldi nest usually consists of several batches of eggs laid by different females. A female is much more likely to lay her eggs in a nest that already has eggs in it than in an empty one. But females like to lay their eggs next to eggs only at a certain stage of development. The eggs darken as they approach hatching and become less attractive to females scouting nests. If a male has a nest with several batches of eggs in the

A male garibaldi damselfish guards his nest of red algae. The algae is not needed to nourish the fish or the eggs, but it requires care similar to that needed by the eggs.

"right" stage of development, and one batch that is too far gone, it is possible that, by eating the darker eggs, he can attract several females to add new eggs to his nest. It's a gamble, but he may end up with many more offspring by sacrificing a few. Still unclear is why female garibaldis prefer to deposit their eggs next to eggs only of a certain age.

Like jawfish, male cardinalfish brood eggs in their mouths and are also known to consume the eggs on occasion. However, in this case, researchers found a direct relationship between how well the fish was fed before it started breeding and the likelihood of its eating eggs. How many batches of eggs the cardinalfish had already brooded also made a difference. Since the fathers are unable to feed while they are brooding eggs, their hunger level increases with each successive batch. Cannibalism in cardinalfish may result simply from a combination of hunger and having an easy meal right in the mouth.

Female octopuses have been known to cannibalize not their offspring or siblings but their mates. Octopuses are promiscuous, form no long-term bonds, and usually die after reproducing. The female will need all the energy she can get while caring for her eggs, since she typically stops feeding as soon as they are laid. Presumably the mate is a source of extra energy. One researcher saw a fe-

83

Opposite: A male garibaldi guards its nest. It will chase away fish much larger than itself and even attack divers. It must also clean and aerate the eggs until they hatch. Above: The female octopus does not feed while guarding the eggs, which are usually attached to the underside of a coral ledge or other hiding place.

The extremely low birthrate resulting from intrauterine cannibalism in the sand tiger shark makes it extremely vulnerable to overfishing. Once populations are reduced by fishing, they recover very slowly, or not at all.

male octopus eat one male, then mate with another only a few minutes later. A common octopus may spend up to three months—a quarter of her life span—aerating and grooming her eggs. During this time she never leaves her den, and she slowly wastes away, dying shortly after the eggs hatch.

CANNIBALS IN THE WOMB. Baby sharks are usually at little risk of being eaten by the father, only because the mother seeks secluded and protected areas to give birth—usually far from where adult sharks feed. They are often, however, at risk from larger juveniles. Baby sand tiger sharks consume their siblings while still in the womb. Sand tigers are born alive from eggs that hatch inside the mother. Unlike those of other sharks, the sand tigers' teeth are fully erupted and ready to use as soon as the embryos hatch from the egg. The first embryo to hatch in each uterus consumes all the other eggs and developing embryos. There is one uterus on each side of the body. Therefore, only two babies are born from each pregnancy. Since sand tigers give birth only every other year, this averages to a reproductive rate of only one offspring per year. Under natural conditions, a low reproductive rate is a good adaptation for top predators such as sharks so that they don't outstrip their resources. However, such species become highly vulnerable to overfishing.

UNDERSEA SUMO WRESTLING. Unlike the closely related squid and cuttlefish and most other invertebrates, octopuses have internal fertilization. Most attach the fertilized eggs to the seafloor within some kind of den that they provide for themselves. A few species brood the embryos on their arms or within their bodies. At least one type gives live birth. Octopuses also differ from their close relatives, and most of the rest of the animal kingdom, in that males do not seem to fight over females. They are mostly solitary, so males may rarely encounter each other, but on occasion, several males have been seen mating or attempting to mate with the same female.

A freshly hatched octopus prepares to leave the nest. Its siblings can be seen, still inside the egg capsules, feeding off the white oval egg yolk.

Courtship among cuttlefish involves a lot of gentle stroking and color changes. The actual mating act occurs very quickly with the male reaching into the female's mantle and depositing a sperm packet.

Squid and cuttlefish are more social, and males may compete fiercely for access to females. In squid, though, the fights are mostly visual. Males compete by flashing vivid color patterns at each other. Cuttlefish also use violent-looking color patterns to ward off male rivals, expanding and contracting pigment sacs on their skin to alter their appearance. Their fights often become very physical, with contestants grappling like undersea sumo wrestlers to toss the opponent away from the female. A male who has just mated with a female will guard her to keep other males away and ensure that it is his sperm that fertilizes her eggs. If a rival succeeds in displacing him, the new suitor may attempt to displace his sperm as well. The victorious male seizes the female and, before mating with her himself, pumps strong jets of water into her mantle to wash out the sperm packets of his predecessor.

SINATRAS OF THE DEEP. Bicolor damselfish compete for mates not by flashing or fighting but with serenades. Although the male damselfish does make an elaborate visual display, including color changes and a little up-and-down dance, it is his chirps that initially attract the female to his territory. Researchers have shown that when female damsels are courted by more than one male, invariably they choose the one with the deepest voice. Since the chirping calls of the dam-

A bicolor damselfish in its normal or resting color phase. During courtship and spawning, the color pattern reverses, with the tail turning black, and the male may display a golden "crown" on the forehead.

selfish are produced by vibrating the swim bladder, and a larger bladder produces a lower-frequency sound, it is always the largest fish that gets the bride.

Humpback whales also sing during mating season, but their songs are much more complex and their purpose is less clear. It is only the males that sing, although the females produce a considerable repertoire of other calls. A humpback whale song is a complex series of calls with a fixed structure. Humpbacks sing the same song every year, with minor changes such as addition or deletion of a verse. And all of the humpbacks in a population

Courtship in humpback whales is a long, involved, and poorly understood process, involving fighting and vocal, visual, and tactile displays. Here a male attempts to stimulate a female by gently blowing bubbles underneath her as she rests near the surface. Bubbles may also be used as an aggressive display between males.

sing the same song. Humpbacks that feed in Alaska during the summer may go to breed in either Mexico or Hawaii in the winter. They don't sing while in Alaska, and yet when they arrive in Hawaii, the males sing essentially the same song as the ones in Mexico 3,000 miles away.

If the humpbacks' purpose in singing is to attract a mate, the endeavor is spectacularly unsuccessful. They often sing for hours or even days without attracting any other whales. When a whale does approach, it is most often another male, who may fight with the singer. It may be that the song is a fighting call or a sort of display of social status or position in the dominance hierarchy of the whale population.

WARM BLOOD IN THE SEA. Whales, dolphins, seals, sea lions, otters, and sea cows, like humans, are warm-blooded, air-breathing mammals. Like us, they have internal fertilization, carry their young for close to a year before giving live birth, nurse the young from mammary glands on the female, and care for them after birth, often for an extended period. Unlike us, marine mammals almost

Spotted dolphins travel in mixed groups. Like humans, but unlike many other animals, they mate throughout the year, regardless of whether or not a female is "in heat" or ovulating.

8
9

Bubble Battles and Sperm Competition

Many whales, notably sperm, gray, and humpback whales, engage in epic battles over mating rights. A female humpback in heat may lead a pack of up to several dozen males on a wild chase during which the males charge each other blowing streams of bubbles, slam each other with their heads and flukes, and leap on top of each other, sometimes inflicting serious injuries. Male sperm whales have been seen with their jaws locked in ferocious fights that scar the combatants for life. Only the victor of these contests wins the right to accompany the female or females.

Humpback whales

Male right whales, on the other hand, actually seem to cooperate with each other during mating. Females resist most mating attempts and may roll belly-up on the surface to make their genitals inaccessible. Males can counter this by working in teams with one or two males at the surface trying to roll the female back over and another waiting underneath to mate with her. They still compete, though, each trying to produce a larger volume of semen than the other whales. Each male tries to pump more semen into the female than the others, washing out the sperm of his competitors. This has led to the evolution of enormous testes in right whales. The combined weight of the two testes can be over a ton—as much as five percent of the total body weight. In this case the winner is usually not the first whale to mate with the female but the last.

never form lifelong monogamous pairs. Most have promiscuous mating systems.

For dolphins and other mammals, sex may serve various social purposes in addition to reproduction. It may be used to reaffirm bonds or to establish dominance. Among dolphins, it occurs so frequently and casually that some researchers quip that for dolphins, sex is like a handshake. Inbreeding is limited by the tendency of male dolphins to roam around and seek mating opportunities with females of other pods, or groups of dolphins.

Males are more successful in these amorous forays if they can procure the assistance of one or more companions. A few buddies are useful both to fight off the resident males and to subdue the female if she is unwilling. Among bottlenose dolphins that have been studied in Australia, forcible abductions of females are not uncommon. Coalitions of young males capture females in heat and take turns mating with them. They sometimes form temporary alliances with other male coalitions in order to defeat rival males or for help with abducting females. They sometimes play rough, and the females may end up covered with rake marks from the sharp teeth of the males.

MALE CHASERS.
It is usually males that compete for the females and not vice versa. This is true even for damselfish, whose males care for the eggs, and sea horses, whose males brood the eggs and bear the young. Male sea horses tail-wrestle and snap at each other when vying for access to females. Curiously, pipefish, which are closely related to sea horses but exhibit less parental care by the male, are one of the rare groups in which females sometimes compete more for the males than the other way around. Another exception is a type of mantis shrimp in which the females aggressively chase the males, attempting to seize

In certain types of mantis shrimp, typical sex roles are reversed, with the female aggressively pursuing the male. This shrimp is of the "smasher" type. The bright yellow forearm ends in a blunt club for smashing prey. Other types of mantis shrimp have sharp claw tips for spearing prey.

Is the spiral tusk on the forehead of the male narwhal a weapon or a decorative ornament? The "fencing contests" between male narwhals seem to be ritualized—rarely involving serious injury to the participants.

them with their razor-sharp claws. The males may be injured by the females before, during, or after mating. A female usually tries to mate with many males before laying each batch of eggs, even though one mating would be adequate to fertilize all the eggs. She may be trying to diversify the genetic makeup of her brood as insurance that some will survive.

UNICORNS AND HAREM MASTERS.

As a result of the competition for mates, males grow much larger than females in many species and may develop elaborate structures for fighting or for impressing the females. The female narwhal, for example, doesn't look too different from any other small whale. But in the male a single tooth erupts through the upper lip and grows to a length of up to ten feet. The spiral tusks are used in ritual sparring contests between males and, at least occasionally, as deadly weapons. In the Middle Ages they were sold as "unicorn horns" and fetched outlandish prices. Sperm whales of both sexes develop teeth in the lower jaw only, but they are apparently used primarily by males during their mating contests. Male sperm whales can weigh up to three times as much as females, grow longer, and develop much larger heads. Enigmatically, female humpback

whales are slightly larger, on average, than the males. Since the males compete violently for access to the females, one would expect size to be a greater advantage for the males.

Size differences between males and females can be extreme for animals whose males fight to control a harem of females. A southern elephant seal male, for example, can weigh four times as much as the female. Imposing size is an advantage in controlling the harem as well as in defending it against rivals—a single male may dominate a harem of up to 1,000 females. Male elephant seals also develop a bulbous proboscis, which is used as a resonator to produce a resounding threat call that, with a visual display, eliminates the need for most of the fighting. A threat may not be enough, however, to restrain a male of similar size. A bloody battle could result in the death of one or both of the combatants. The harem master does not feed for two to three months while defending his territory,

Left: *Male narwhals lift their tusks in ritualized displays during the mating season, often knocking them together in sparring matches that can result in broken tusks and head scars. The tusks can reach ten feet in length, with a circumference of more than eight inches at the base, and can weigh more than 20 pounds.*
Below: *A bull elephant seal is much larger than the female underneath him. Males need to attain a large size to establish their harems and defend them from other males.*

and the fighting and starvation take their toll. Rarely does a bull manage to retain his dominance for more than two or three years, and most die within a couple of years of their best breeding season.

Harem-type breeding systems are not restricted to mammals. Assorted varieties of fishes, including triggerfish and some wrasses, breed in harems. Some of these harems are in permanent territories, while some fishes establish leks, which are temporary territories defended by a male solely for the purpose of breeding, as terrestrial animals such as elks do. Male triggerfish defend their nests with a ferocity that makes some of them a hazard to divers during the breeding season. Some kinds of triggerfish can reach a size of two feet and can draw blood and even remove flesh with a bite.

NOT ALL MALES ARE LARGER. Gender-related size differences among fishes are more difficult to understand than those among mammals. In many fishes, including the blue marlin and the white shark, the female is significantly larger than the male. In others the male is larger. Wrasses and parrotfish have two types of males, one of which is identical to the female and the other which is much larger and differently colored. And in many other fishes, males and females grow to about the same size and may be identical in appearance. It is sometimes explained that when the fish reach sexual maturity, the females have to put more

Opposite: *Triggerfish get their name from the second dorsal spine. When the triggerfish dives into a coral crevice, it erects the large first spine, locking the fish into its hiding place. The fish can be removed only by pressing on the second spine, or "trigger," which releases the first spine.* Above: *The male great white shark (pictured here) is smaller than the female. Very little is known about the reproduction of white sharks.*

Dwarf Parasitic Mates

Finding a mate in the ocean depths can be a real problem. Since food resources are relatively scarce in the abyss, animals tend to be spaced far apart. Individuals that fail to find a mate are eliminated from the gene pool.

Some organisms have solved this problem in unique ways. Males of a certain deep-sea anglerfish are only a few thousandths the weight of females. When a male locates a female, by following her scent, he attaches himself to her side with a bite. He then fuses to her body and begins to degenerate. Eventually the male is reduced to little more than a small amount of gonadal tissue nourished by the female's bloodstream. The male's only function is to produce sperm to fertilize the female's eggs. Neither partner will ever have to look for a mate again. The female may, however, accept additional sex partners, providing they are willing to offer a lifetime commitment.

Deep-sea anglerfish

energy into egg production than the males have to expend on sperm. This allows the males to invest more energy in growth. The mystery is why this does not apply to those species in which the female grows larger.

WHERE DO THE EGGS GO? Another mystery involves the destiny of the eggs and larvae. Where do the eggs that are released into the water end up? Do all of a fish's offspring go somewhere down-current? The powerful Gulf Stream current system sweeps through the West Indies before rounding Florida and continuing up the east coast of the United States. Does this inexorable flow cause most of the marine life in Florida to depend upon spawning activity in the Caribbean? Is all the reproductive activity on Florida reefs wasted as the eggs are swept north into waters too cold for the survival of the offspring? What about the fish of isolated oceanic islands? Are all of their eggs lost into the vastness of the ocean? How can they populate their reefs with only the eggs or larvae that survive the crossing from the next island upstream?

Research has shown that many fish in such situations select the time and location of spawning to take advantage of circular currents and eddies, such as the ones that are created on the down-current side of oceanic islands during spring tides. Spawning on strong ebb tides carries the eggs away from the reef and the many hungry mouths that might consume them there. A circular current ensures that some larvae are brought back to the reef after a period of development at sea. Many isolated oceanic islands are home to endemic fish species — varieties found only in that location and nowhere else. This is convincing evidence of reproductive isolation. Even in Florida, which certainly receives some input from upstream breeding, genetic research is showing that some populations are largely self-seeding.

GLOBE-TROTTERS. Many whales, like seals and sea lions, return year after year to the same locations to mate and bear their young. The migrations they undertake to reach the breeding grounds are among the greatest animal migrations known. Gray whales may swim more than 6,000 miles between their summer and winter homes. Most whales feed little, or not at all, during long migrations and while on the breeding grounds, often living for months on energy stored in

A baby gray whale lifts its head above the water in a breeding lagoon along the coast of Baja California. After a month or two nursing from its mother and gaining strength, it will accompany her back to the feeding grounds in the Bering Sea—a journey of 6,000 miles.

A sockeye salmon struggles up a rapids toward the spawning grounds. Salmon feed little, if at all, during their return to freshwater, while expending enormous amounts of energy overcoming the obstacles in their path.

their blubber. The blubber serves for insulation as well as for food storage, which may be why the whales travel so far from where their dinner is served. Most of the feeding grounds are in high latitudes where plankton and schooling fish are abundant, but the water is very cold. Newborn whales, although weighing more than a ton in some species, have only a relatively thin layer of blubber. This may be inadequate to insulate them against the cold waters of the feeding grounds. Generally, in their breeding grounds the water is warmer and calmer, where the young are more likely to survive.

TO REPRODUCE AND DIE. Market squid also appear in the same location each year to reproduce, but it is not the same individuals that come each year to lay their eggs. After a frenzy of mating and egg-laying, carpeting the seafloor with white egg capsules, both male and female squid fall to the bottom themselves and become food for scavenging organisms. Most other varieties of squid, octopus, and cuttlefish also reproduce only once and then die.

This pattern is also shared by such diverse organisms as freshwater eels and salmon. For salmon, the reason is fairly easy to understand. They must leave the ocean, where their food supply is, and fight their way up a river, leaping up rapids and waterfalls and braving grizzly bears and other predators to the very headwaters in order to breed. After expending massive amounts of energy in this journey, and yet more in egg production by the females and fighting by the males, the chances of surviving the return trip are very low. By the end of the spawning run, the bodies of the fish degenerate to the point that they are literally rotting while still alive. Also, the clear streams and lakes where the salmon nest harbor few nutrients for the young to feed on. The adults can best ensure their contribution to future generations by leaving what is left of their bodies in the headwaters. The nutrients released by their rotting bodies nourish tiny aquatic organisms that supply food for the salmon hatchlings.

After hatching in the mountain streams and lakes of North America, Pacific salmon follow their natal river to the ocean. They may cross the Pacific to Japan and back before starting upriver again to breed, placing them in the world league of migrators. While this is a long and costly pilgrimage in order to reproduce, the payoff is clear. The ocean is full of hungry predators that would eagerly devour the young salmon at every stage of their development. The freshwater where the fish actually breed are relatively much safer for the juvenile fish.

Sockeye salmon adopt brilliant red spawning colors as they migrate upstream to reproduce and die. In the ocean these salmon are a dull silver-gray color.

Fish out of Water

Grunion not only leave the ocean to spawn—they leave the water entirely. On the Pacific coast of North America, these fish wait until the last of the high spring tides that follow the full and new moons. Then, just as the tide begins to fall, they flop up onto the beach. The female digs her tail into the sand and deposits her eggs, while males coil around her and fertilize them. The eggs develop during the period of lower tides that follows. At the next full or new moon, when the high tide reaches the eggs again, they hatch and the larvae enter the ocean. Sea turtles and horseshoe crabs are other marine animals that leave the ocean to lay their eggs on the beach. Although the eggs are protected from being eaten by fish and other ocean predators, they are exposed to attack by birds, raccoons, dogs, and other predators who appeared later in the evolutionary process.

Grunion spawning on a beach

INCREDIBLE JOURNEY. Other fish undertake a spawning migration in the reverse direction from salmon. Freshwater eels in the rivers of North America and Europe migrate downstream to the ocean when they reach maturity. They then undertake a journey that seems almost incomprehensible, swimming nearly all the way around the North Atlantic before arriving at a remote location in the Sargasso Sea, between Bermuda and Puerto Rico. Here they spawn, at depths of 1,300 to 2,500 feet, and die. The larvae, when they hatch, must complete the circle to return to the rivers where they will live as adults. The trip can take one to three years. Some of them climb all the way to the upper valleys of the Alps. When they encounter a waterfall too steep to climb, they leave the river and slither upstream through the vegetation at its edge.

With all the hazards facing the tiny larvae in the open ocean, and during the return migration upstream, why should eels adopt such an unlikely life history? The answer may be that it is more of a historical accident than an adaptive strategy. Marine eels may have begun to colonize freshwater habitats at a time when the American and European continents were very close together. Although the eels were able to survive and feed in freshwater, they may not have been able to make the necessary physiological adaptations to reproduce there. When the Atlantic Ocean was only a narrow strip of water separating the two continents, it wouldn't have been much of a journey from a river mouth in either continent to the center of the ocean. As continental drift pushed the continents farther apart, the eels may have gradually adapted by lengthening their migration. Nonetheless, their choice of spawning locations may offer survival value: The waters of the Sargasso Sea are low in productivity and contain fewer egg-eating and larvae-eating crea-

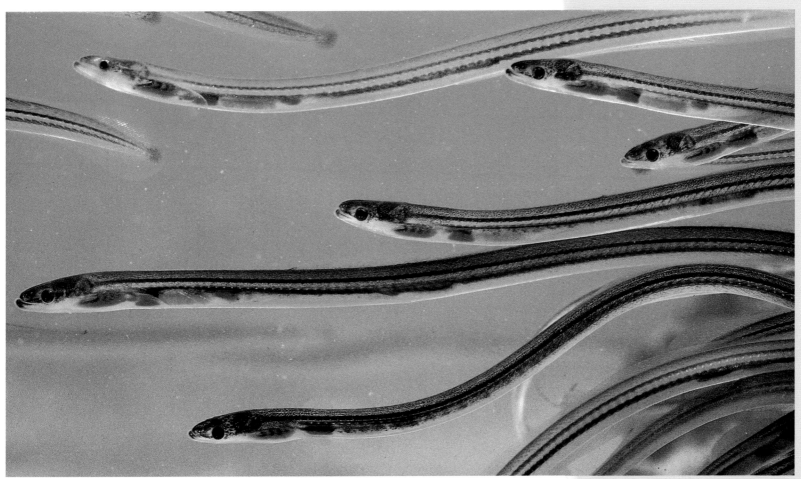

tures than do the coastal waters of the Atlantic. This may be especially true at the great depths where the eels breed.

Many other questions have yet to be answered. Unlike individual salmon, which return to the place of their "birth" by memory of its smell or taste, baby eels have never been in a river and have no such memory. How do they find their way there, and how do the adults navigate back to the spawning grounds, traveling at depths of over 1,000 feet? Do the eels find their mates in the river and make the journey in tandem, or do they meet their mates in the Sargasso Sea?

Above: *When the eel larvae finally reach the mouth of a river, after a migration of thousands of miles, they metamorphose into elvers like these.* Left: *When freshwater eels spawn in the Sargasso Sea, they produce leptocephalus larvae like this one. The flimsy, nearly transparent, ribbonlike larvae must travel thousands of miles through the open ocean over a one- to three-year period before reaching the mouth of a stream or river.*

CLONES AND IMMORTALITY.

In the sea, as ashore, many organisms do not bother with sex or even with sex cells such as eggs. Billions of bacteria and other simple organisms reproduce quite efficiently by simply splitting in half. Other creatures reproduce both sexually and asexually. Sponges, anemones, and corals may replicate themselves by just budding off another individual (a clone), by splitting into two or more individuals, by producing asexual seedlike structures, or by a variety of sexual techniques.

The small flowerlike buds on the stalk of this sea anemone will eventually detach and become free-living animals. Each will be a clone — genetically identical to the parent anemone. Anemones can also reproduce sexually.

The regenerative powers of sponges are legend. If a sponge is forced through a mesh, the separated cells will reorganize themselves into several new sponges. Sponges broken into small pieces can grow into many new sponges. Some corals also have this ability. Some kinds of staghorn coral thrive in hurricane-prone and wave-tossed environments due to their ability to spread and multiply when shattered into pieces.

An individual that can renew itself by cloning and/or regeneration could potentially live forever. However, over time, an accumulation of random genetic mutations eventually kills off some lineages while driving others along new paths of evolution. Sexual reproduction may have evolved partly as a way of dividing up mutations among the offspring, allowing those that received the "bad" mutant genes to die off and those that received the "good" mutations to evolve and prosper. In theory, sexless cloning should leave a population vulnerable to extinction in the face of changing environmental conditions. Sexual reproduction, by shuffling genes, is supposed to provide greater genetic variability and greater adaptability. But some of the ostracods may have been

Split Personalities

Most sea stars reproduce sexually. Upon receiving the proper environmental cue, a star rises up as if on the tips of its toes and releases gametes from the gonads on the undersides of its arms. A few species are hermaphroditic, but in most, individuals are either male or female. Usually the stimulant for spawning is the release of gametes by a member of the opposite sex. But that brings up a question: What stimulates the first individual in an area?

At least 19 species of sea stars reproduce both sexually and asexually. Asexual reproduction is by fission. The two halves of the star simply stretch apart, leaving

Sea star regenerating

a narrow strip of tissue connecting the parts, and eventually separate. Each half then regenerates the missing portion. Some local populations of stars reproduce by fission only, never bothering with sex.

Sea stars can also regenerate parts lost to predation. They may even deliberately cast off an arm to escape a predator. In most species, a piece as small as one arm and one-fifth of the central disk can regenerate an entire new body. In one genus of sea stars, a single arm is all that is needed.

reproducing without fertilization for the last 70 million years.

UNDERSEA BLIZZARD.

Depending on the species, sponges, anemones, and corals may either have separate males and females or be hermaphroditic. Some species brood the fertilized eggs within their bodies, but other species release eggs and sperm into the ocean. The release of eggs or sperm by one individual can trigger release by a neighbor, and on down the line, until the entire reef is "smoking," with nearly every member of the species pumping its reproductive products into the water.

On some reefs various species coordinate their reproductive activity in mass spawning events. On the Great Barrier Reef in Australia, during several consecutive nights following a full moon of late spring or early summer, more than 130 species of coral and dozens of species of other organisms from sea stars to worms all discharge their gametes into the water in a great cloud. The spawning takes place synchronously across hundreds of miles of reef. The eggs and larvae float to the surface, forming slicks up to several miles long, which are clearly visible and often mistaken for oil spills.

Opposite: *A healthy coral reef is a community of hard corals, soft corals, various kinds of fish, and many other organisms. The life cycles of all these creatures are dependent upon each other. Even the act of reproduction may be coordinated among a large number of unrelated organisms.*

Above: *A sponge releases eggs in a gelatinous matrix. The eggs will be fertilized by sperm arriving in the current from other sponges. Opposite: A brown sponge releasing sperm. Chemical signals from this sponge will trigger the next sponge down-current to begin spawning as well. This will continue until the whole reef is "smoking."*

How all these disparate organisms synchronize their reproductive activity has yet to be fully explained, but all of the participants reap clear advantages. Coral reefs are rife with nest robbers. Fishes such as wrasses and fusiliers are voracious egg predators. By spawning at night, when many of the egg eaters are asleep, the risk can be reduced.

But other fish are active at night, even swimming in from offshore waters to take part in the feast. However, the sheer volume of reproductive output swamps the feasters, producing what biologists call "predator saturation." Each organism reduces the chance that its eggs will be eaten by spawning at the same time as other organisms. Various species spawn at different times throughout the night. Somehow, through chemical cues and by precision timing, the eggs and sperm manage to sort it all out and unite (mostly) with their own species. Somehow, they also usually manage to avoid "selfing," or uniting with gametes from the same individual that spawned them. Such an intricate coordination of the life histories of hundreds of species and millions of individuals is awe inspiring, and the spectacle is one of the true wonders of the natural world.

Wriggling Delicacies

A group of segmented worms known as palolo worms stage their own mass spawning events. In the Samoan Islands, these worms are numerous, but they usually stay hidden in burrows in the reef. When it is time to spawn, however, the worm is of two minds about this habit. One half wants to stay safely buried in the bottom, while the other half wants to rise to the surface to partake in a great writhing orgy. So they split in two—the part with the brains staying safely on the bottom and the part with the gonads wriggling up to the giddy rendezvous above. If left to their own devices, the millions of tail-ends wriggle about until the first light of day and then dissolve into an oily slick of eggs and sperm, which unite to initiate a new generation.

However, it is the custom of the Samoans not to leave the palolo worms to their own devices. On the appointed evening, every man, woman, and child not in sickbed is down at the seashore scooping the squirming brown and green vermicelli into buckets. If the spawn is good, all will partake of the delicacy. If the spawn is poor, only the chiefs will dine. Since the timing of the spawn can be predicted, using the solar and lunar calendars, gourmets routinely fly to Samoa from as far away as New York and Paris for the event. The palolo worms are eaten raw, boiled, fried, or steamed, and they have a delicate flavor that is said to be an acquired taste.

Jaws and Claws

The male bicolor damselfish arises before dawn to attend to one of the two activities most vital to any creature: reproduction. He carefully tends his nest, nipping away any algae that may have intruded upon the clean surface awaiting a fresh batch of eggs. At first light, he emerges from the burrow and begins to broadcast his mating call. A series of three quick chirps advertises his readiness to mate with any female that will have him. Nearby, a female damselfish emerges from her burrow.

A cloud of small damselfish rises into the water column to feed on plankton and drifting food particles.

Above: *The bicolor damselfish is a plankton feeder. It normally stays close to the bottom, but the male may swoop up as high as four feet during its courtship display. Opposite: A trumpetfish assumes a vertical orientation to match the gorgonian branches it is using for cover. In natural light it would match the coral's color, but the artificial light of the photographer's strobe brings out its red color.*

She listens to the insistent chirping of the male damselfish and carefully analyzes the call, trying to determine if he will be a suitable mate to fertilize and care for her eggs.

Not far away, another fish is also listening carefully. The long, slender trumpetfish is not interested in sex, however. It is attending to the other activity of utmost significance to any living thing: getting a meal. Sea animals, like forest animals, routinely eavesdrop on any communications of other species that may provide them useful information. Sensing an opportunity, the trumpetfish moves stealthily forward into the branches of a purplish-gray bushlike gorgonian coral, swaying gently in the ocean surge. The trumpetfish rotates into a vertical orientation, with its head down and body parallel to the branches of the soft coral. It drifts back and forth in the surge, matching the movement of the coral branches.

LOVE'S SACRIFICE. The female damselfish decides that the voice she hears belongs to a suitable partner. She begins to move in the direction of the male's burrow. Seeing her approaching, the male begins a series of acrobatic maneuvers. He rolls on his side, then swoops up in a steep vertical climb. Reaching the apex of his ascent at a point about four feet above his burrow, he brakes and starts his turn to the descent. At that instant, however, his world suddenly turns dark, and he feels a constricting pressure on all sides of his body.

The trumpetfish, observing the male's distraction as the female approached, had slowly tilted down to a horizontal orientation, with its arrowlike body pointed directly above the damselfish. As the damsel reached the upper part of his courtship rush, the trumpetfish gave two quick lateral beats of the rear part of its body and shot forward like a guided missile. At a distance of a few inches from the damsel, the body of the trumpetfish abruptly changed shape. All of the bones of the jaws suddenly separated from each other and exploded outward, connected by only a thin transparent membrane. The slender body that had moments before been indistinguishable from the supple branches of the gorgonian had ballooned at one end into the shape of a trumpet bell.

In rapidly expanding to more than 50 times its previous volume, the mouth of the trumpetfish created a powerful suction. Even as the jaws move forward

to envelop the space where the damselfish had been, the damsel was irresistibly sucked into the mouth and drawn down into the gullet of the trumpetfish. The female damsel does not see all of this, however. Such is the speed of the attack that all she experiences is a brief flash of color, an unexpected pressure wave passing through the water, and the mysterious disappearance of her suitor. Unsettled by the abrupt cancellation of the courtship, she returns to her burrow and, for the next half hour, does not respond to the strident triple chirps of the other males in the vicinity.

The trumpetfish has gained only a brief respite from the death sentence hanging over its own head. As a predator, it must kill to live. If it fails to make another successful attack that day, its energy and protein needs will not be met. If

A trumpetfish has just seized a damselfish, which can be seen through the semitransparent sides of the trumpetfish's mouth.

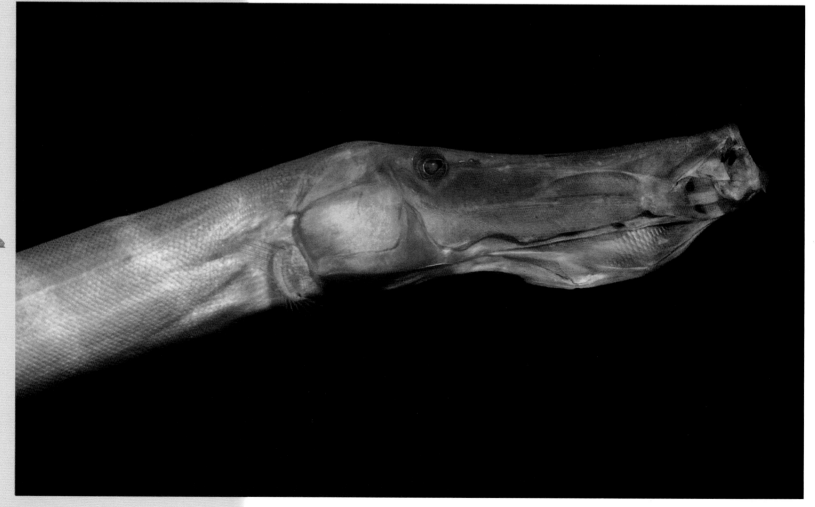

A pair of trumpetfish try to meld with a tiger grouper in this rare photo. The grouper gains nothing from the association and may attempt to ditch the trumpetfish by ducking through coral overhangs or other obstacles.

it has a week of poor hunting, the sentence will be executed. To survive in the ocean wilderness, a predator needs all the skills the trumpetfish has so ably demonstrated: blinding speed, cunning, stealth, acute senses, and a comprehensive knowledge of the habits and signals of its potential prey.

DIRTY TRICKS. Most predator species have a unique bag of tricks that give them an edge in the brutal struggle for survival. One of the trumpetfish's remarkable habits is a technique known as shadow stalking. The trumpetfish contours its slim, flexible body to the shape of a larger fish roaming the reef. Swimming so

Underwater Anglers

Frogfish, batfish, and other types of anglerfishes use, in addition to highly effective camouflage, a sneaky trick to snare their unwary prey. On top of the head sits a tiny fishing pole with a fleshy lure at the end. The fishing pole has evolved from the first spine of the dorsal fin on the fish's back. The anglerfish jigs the lure back and forth to mimic the motion of a small planktonic animal. When a fish comes to investigate the enticing morsel, the would-be diner suddenly vanishes down the angler's throat instead. Anglerfish have expandable abdomens and can swallow fish larger than themselves. In deep-sea anglerfishes, the lure is luminous, to mimic the light-emitting shrimp and other creatures found in the ocean depths. Other deep-sea creatures, such as the cookie-cutter shark, have luminous tissue in the linings of their mouths, to actually lure their dinner right inside their jaws.

close to the body of its host that it is indistinguishable from it, the trumpetfish follows its host's every movement. The host is usually a grouper or other large predator that takes much larger prey than a trumpetfish does. The small fish that the trumpetfish preys upon are not concerned when they see the grouper. Its body is not designed to capture such tiny morsels. Suddenly, however, part of its body appears to peel away from the rest and is upon them before they realize what has happened. At other times, the trumpetfish hangs motionless in a cluster of tube sponges, gorgonians, or other elongated objects that conceal its long, skinny body. When a prey item passes close enough, the trumpetfish darts forward and seizes it.

This "lurk and lunge" strategy is used effectively by a number of reef fish, including groupers, lizardfish, toadfish, frogfish, batfish, and sea horses. A grouper can remain motionless in a cave entrance or other place of concealment for hours or even days. When another fish passes by, there is a quick lunge, and the cavernous mouth opens

A jewfish, weighing hundreds of pounds, can "inhale" an average-sized reef fish into its enormous mouth faster than the human eye can follow. A loud "bang" indicates that its jaws have opened and closed, and at that instant the prey fish seems to simply disappear.

and expands so rapidly that all the water in front of it is sucked inside, fish included. The larger grouper species, known as jewfish and giant sea bass, can grow to over 600 pounds. When one of these fish feeds, the rapid opening and closing of the mouth creates an underwater thunderclap so loud that it sounds as

if a powerful firecracker has gone off. The action occurs so quickly that a human eye cannot follow it. All an observer sees is that a fish that was in front of the jewfish has suddenly disappeared.

Some lurking predators enhance their effectiveness with camouflage that makes them appear to be part of the reef. Scorpionfish and stonefish, for example, grow fleshy flaps all over their heads and bodies that make them appear like an algae-covered rock. Frogfish have evolved lumpy bodies resembling in both form and texture the sponges they usually hide on. They also have the ability to change their color to match perfectly the color of their home sponge.

Cuttlefish use their incredible ability to control their skin colors and patterns not only for camouflage but also to confuse and intimidate their prey. Ap-

A frogfish appears like a lump of sponge on the reef—until it opens its mouth and ingests its prey, which can be nearly as large as the frogfish itself. A tiny fishing lure on a filament attached to the head of the frogfish is used to attract the prey.

A lionfish hovers near a sea fan. The lacy, poison-tipped fins are used to herd and corner small prey.

proaching a crab, a cuttlefish may adopt what is known as a "passing cloud" pattern. Waves of dark and light bands pass from one end of the cuttlefish's body to the other. As it slowly moves toward the crab, the waves of color race faster and faster across its body. The crab appears to be mesmerized by the astonishing display and remains motionless as the cuttlefish edges closer and closer. When it reaches striking distance, the cuttlefish merely reaches down with a tentacle and snatches up the hypnotized crab.

Lionfish, also known as turkey fish, also confuse both larger predators and prey with their banded camouflage pattern. But they have another trick up their sleeves as well. They spread open their wide, winglike pectoral fins and use them to herd small fish or shrimp into a corner where they can be captured. In some species, parts of the membrane between the rays supporting the fin are transparent. The panicked prey fish may attempt to dash through one of these "openings," only to be caught and swept back toward the lionfish's mouth.

SPEARS AND CLUBS. Mantis shrimps rely not on tricks but on speed. Though very similar in appearance to their namesakes, the praying mantises, these shrimps are not insects but crustaceans. Like the insects, they keep their raptorial arms folded up against their bodies. The muscles that extend the strik-

This mantis shrimp is of the "smasher" type. Its claws are modified to form blunt clubs at the "elbows" for knocking its prey senseless and for smashing open shells.

ing arms are tensed in preparation for a strike, but the arms are held in the folded position by click joints. When the joints are popped open and the tension is released, the arms extend much more quickly than the muscles could extend them by a normal contraction. A strike can be

completed in less than five milliseconds. A mantis shrimp's strike is one of the fastest actions in the animal kingdom.

There are two types of mantis shrimps. "Spearers" impale their prey on sharply pointed claws. "Smashers" have rounded clublike tips on their appendages instead of sharp points. Their blow is just as fast, is extremely powerful, and can knock a victim dead or unconscious or crack its shell open.

SUPERSTARS.

Two "smasher" mantis shrimp fight for control of a burrow. One shrimp uses its tail to deflect the blows of the other.

Many sea stars, or starfish, use not speed but patience to overpower their prey. They feed primarily on mussels, clams, and oysters. A sea star grips the shell of a mussel on both sides with the suction cups on the ends of its tube feet and begins to pull. The mussel is stronger. Few things can pull its shell open. But it lacks the endurance of the sea star. The star continues to pull for hours, if necessary, until the mussel tires. Once it has been able to create a gap of as little as a tenth of a millimeter, the star begins to extrude its stomach into the oyster's shell. Other kinds of sea stars use their tube feet to chip away the lip of the shell until they have created a small opening. Either way, the sea star's stomach comes out of its mouth and inside the shell of its prey. If it is attacking a sea snail, with a single spiral shell instead of two, the sea star's stomach snakes its way through the opening and around the whorls of the shell. The stomach lining secretes enzymes that dissolve the flesh of its victim, which is then absorbed into the lining. The process continues over a period of hours until nothing is left but a smooth, shiny shell.

Some sea stars swallow their prey whole. A giant sun star can swallow an entire prickly sea urchin. But the stomach lining still has to enter the shell of the food item before it can be digested. After digestion the empty shell is regurgitated back out the mouth.

Some starfish feed on detritus and microorganisms. One type swallows mud and absorbs nutrients from the organic matter it contains. The crown-of-thorns sea star feeds almost exclusively on coral. Periodically great plagues of these many-armed starfish

Left: A sea star closes its body around a mussel. The tube feet on the star's legs grip the shell of the mussel and exert a constant pull on it until the shell opens just a fraction. Below: This purple crown-of-thorns sea star is found in the Andaman Sea. The brown coral on one side is still alive, whereas the white portion has been killed by the sea star's feeding on it.

swarm across coral reefs in the Pacific, killing vast areas of reef and leaving behind only empty white skeletons. The goose-foot starfish has not yet been observed feeding, but only fast-moving animals, such as swimming crabs, have been found in its stomach. How it captures these remains a mystery.

VARIED DIET. Sea stars themselves are vulnerable to predation by a number of organisms, regardless of their unappetizing appearance. Triton trumpet shells eat large starfish, including the spiny, venomous crown-of-thorns. Brittle stars are a favorite food of the sand tilefish in the Caribbean. In the Pacific, large sea stars

Opposite: *A crown-of-thorns sea star eats away the living tissue of a coral, leaving behind a bleached white skeleton.* Above: *The harlequin shrimp, or painted prawn, preys on sea urchins and sea stars, which are often much larger than itself. Here one is dining on a sea star that it has dragged back to its lair in the coral.*

Shocking Habits

The lumpy shape and downturned mouth of the stargazer are similar to those of the frogfish. But the form of this fish is rarely visible, because it normally lies on the bottom, buried in the sand, with only its eyes protruding above the surface. When a suitable prey passes overhead, it is stunned by a jolt of current from the stargazer's electric organs and snatched up in a flurry of sand.

Electric rays and torpedo rays use the same trick, lying motionless on the bottom, often either partly or completely buried. Some torpedo rays can generate over 220 volts—enough to electrocute their prey or possibly knock a diver unconscious. Some of them actively stalk their quarry by creeping along the bottom or drifting slowly over the reef.

are attacked by tiny harlequin shrimp (painted prawns). A pair of these beautifully patterned little crustaceans may assault a starfish hundreds of times their size, amputate one of the arms, and drag it back to their den where they can dine on it for an extended period. This activity could more accurately be termed parasitism than predation, since the starfish is able to regenerate the arm and survive. Smaller stars are not so fortunate; they may be dragged whole into the den and consumed in their entirety.

Walruses mostly feed on the same sorts of shellfish as sea stars do. But the popular belief that they use their three-foot-long tusks to dig clams out of the bottom mud is probably not true. Scientists believe that they swim along the bottom feeling for food items with their sensitive whiskers and sucking them up when encountered. A walrus can consume as many as 6,000 clams in a single session. They also consume fish, crabs, worms, shrimp, and snails. Some walruses do use their tusks for taking food. Certain individuals switch to a diet of seals and small whales.

POISON DARTS. Among the deadliest animals in the ocean are the beautiful little cone shells, a type of marine snail. Most are only two to four inches long.

Their shells are covered with intricate patterns that make them a favorite of shell collectors, and the rarer specimens bring high prices. Some collectors pay the ultimate price. Collectors have been killed when a mesh bag containing a live cone shell

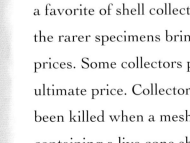

A cone shell crawls across the reef at night, hunting for prey. The venomous dart is carried at the narrow end of the shell, just behind the proboscis. The most likely victim is a sleeping fish.

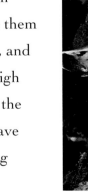

Carrier of one of the deadliest venoms known, the geography cone shell has been responsible for several dozen human deaths. It feeds on fish and occasionally mollusks, stinging its prey to subdue it before engulfing it.

brushed against their skin, allowing the snail to inject them with a venomous dart—actually a hollow tooth—carried on its proboscis. The proboscis is extensible and flexible, permitting the cone shell to attack in any direction.

While some cone shells prey on other snails, worms, and other bottom dwellers, the most dangerous are fish eaters. Some take fish larger than themselves. In order to capture the fish, the cone shell has to paralyze it before the fish can break off the delicate "harpoon line" attaching the poison dart to the snail. Therefore these cones pack multiple nerve toxins that act together to produce instant muscular paralysis when injected into a fish. The proboscis then extends forward and expands to engulf the fish. Most cone shells hide under bottom rubble by day and hunt at night when their prey cannot see them.

VENOMOUS FANGS. Sea snakes are reptiles, descended from land snakes that adapted to life in the water. They must come to the surface to breathe air. Some species are adapted to oceanic life and give live birth to their young at sea. Others come ashore to rest, mate, and lay their eggs. All depend upon the sea for their food, which consists mostly of fish, eels, fish eggs, and shrimp.

Like some of their terrestrial relatives, sea snakes use venom to quickly immobilize their prey. The venom is chemically similar to cobra venom and is injected through fangs structurally similar to the fangs of cobras. However, the venom of sea snakes can be at least four times more toxic than cobra venom. In

An olive sea snake injects venom into a fish to subdue it before attempting to swallow it. With its small mouth and short fangs set in the rear of the mouth, this snake poses little threat to humans.

fact, some sea snake venoms are among the deadliest poisons found in nature.

Most human injuries have occurred when fishermen have handled snakes while removing fish from their nets. Many of these bites have been fatal. The sea snake varieties most likely to be encountered by swimmers, snorkelers, and scuba divers are mild-tempered and have short fangs set far back in the mouth. They also have a very small gape, which hinders biting something as large as a human even if the snake were so inclined.

Beautiful but Lethal

Octopuses can deliver venom through a bite delivered with the beak in the middle of the underside of the body. The venom of most species of octopus is mild, but one species, the blue-ringed octopus, carries a venom that can kill a person in minutes. This three-inch-long, inoffensive-looking creature is normally inconspicuous in its drab brownish coloration. But when it becomes excited, brilliant blue rings flash on its body. In this state, it is extremely dangerous. Its beak is so small that some human victims did not even realize that they had been bitten—usually while playing with the "cute" little octopus. Like its larger relatives, the blue-ringed octopus feeds mostly on crabs, lobsters, and other crustaceans. Yet estimates claim it carries enough poison to kill ten men. Why it needs such a potent venom is not clear.

Blue-ringed octopus

Sea snakes are relatively slow swimmers and would not be able to chase down most of the fish they prey upon. Some snakes specialize in trapping fish such as eels and jawfish in their burrows. Others try to catch fish when they are sleeping or resting inside the reef structure. One kind of sea snake eats nothing but fish eggs and through evolution has lost the ability to produce venom. Sea snakes themselves are preyed upon by sharks and by sea eagles, which track the snakes from high above the water and dive down to snatch them from the surface when they come up to breathe. How the eagles avoid being bitten by their deadly prey while they carry it back to their roost is not known.

SINUOUS FISH. Marine eels have a snakelike appearance and impressive fanglike dentition. But they are fish, not reptiles. They do not inject venom, but their mouths contain bacteria that can cause dangerous infections in the jagged wounds created by their bites. Sea snakes are often seen hunting by day, but eels are almost exclusively nocturnal. They feed mainly upon sleeping fishes that they locate by an extraordinary sense of smell. Their sinuous bodies are capable of weaving through the reef, penetrating tiny openings, and locating even the best-hidden fish. They are capable of swallowing fish much larger than the width of their bodies. In order to gain a purchase on a struggling fish, they sometimes perform a remarkable trick. An eel will tie its body into a knot and pull its head back through the knot until it can use the sides of the knot to brace the fish against.

"Viper worms" have a milder venom than sea snakes and are not known to have ever attacked humans. But they are able predators. These worms, which can grow to a length of eight feet or more, can concentrate metal ions from seawater into their jaws until the jaws are hardened into nearly pure metal. The terminal end of the worm consists of a mouth surrounded by a ring of sensory tentacles. When the tentacles detect the movement of prey, the jaws evert and are fired out of the body to seize the victim. Poison glands next to the jaws then pump venom into it. Fortunately, these worms are mostly nocturnal and prefer shallow, muddy bottoms not frequented by sport divers.

Above: *The dragon moray, or leopard eel, is one of the more unusual marine eels. The hornlike projections on the head, bright colors, and exposed teeth give it a ferocious appearance, but it is shy and retiring toward divers. Opposite: Jellyfish use their long, dangling tentacles like fishing lines. But instead of a baited hook, the tentacles are armed with miniature poisoned harpoons.*

STINGERS. The venom of corals and anemones and their kin, the sea jellies and hydroids, is generally not highly toxic to humans, although some people have allergic reactions. Their stinging weapons are delicate little hairlike structures,

Delicate and Deadly

In the group of animals that includes the corals and anemones, sea jellies and hydroids have the most potent toxins. The most deadly is the box jellyfish found near Australia. Its sting is so powerful that if a tentacle crosses a swimmer's chest, it can stop the heart, causing instant death. Humans who survive an encounter with this predator usually suffer excruciating pain and permanent scarring. The delicate-looking, transparent box jellyfish feeds on fish that are both faster and stronger than the jellies are. So that the jelly won't be damaged by the fish's struggles, it needs a potent venom that will paralyze a fish on contact.

During the summer months, box jellyfish often gather in large numbers off beaches in the northern part of Australia, causing the beaches to be unsafe for swimming. At the end of the summer the jellyfish reproduce. The larval stage passes the winter hiding on the bottom in estuaries and tidal creeks before reemerging the following summer as a voracious and deadly predator.

The Portuguese man-of-war is the second most lethal of the sea jellies. It also has caused a number of human fatalities. It is actually a colonial hydroid composed of many individuals that work together as a single superorganism. Its jellyfishlike surface float enables it to travel the oceans by wind propulsion.

Part of its menace is due to its stinging tentacles, which can trail as long as 50 feet from the float and are nearly invisible in the water. Each tentacle belongs to an individual animal. They are used much like fishing lines. When a fish is captured, the tentacles holding it are drawn in, the fish is passed to one of the stomachs for digestion, and the fishing lines are lowered again.

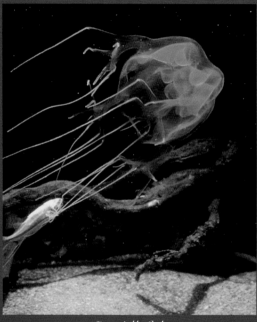

Box jellyfish

usually less than one millimeter long. Very often the stingers are not even long enough to pierce a human's skin, but they can be quite deadly to the creatures these animals feed on. And what they lack in potency they more than make up in numbers. A victim may be pierced with thousands of harpoonlike stingers.

The stingers are shaped like inverted tubes and are coiled in the tips of the tentacles. When prey brushes against the tentacles, the tubes are fired outward, turning inside out as they are forced out. The hollow tip pierces the victim's skin on contact, and venom is pumped into its body. When the soft body of a planktonic worm touches the tentacles of a coral, the combined assault of a large number of harpoons striking at once can cause it to explode. Most corals stick to feeding on plankton, but some anemones can kill and devour fish. One writer described seeing a foot-

long fish stopped cold when it brushed against the tentacles of a large anemone, which then consumed it.

WORKING TOGETHER.

Many creatures improve their hunting success by working together. Bluefin tuna have been seen hunting in a V formation, with all members of the pack evenly spaced to maximize the chances of encountering prey. If a school of fish is found, the tuna close ranks and circle the smaller fish to keep them packed into a tight ball that the tuna can feed on.

Sailfish and marlin sometimes work a school of small fish in the same way. While the rest of the marlin continue to circle the bait ball to keep it tightly packed, one or two swim through the center swinging their bills back and forth to kill or stun the bait fish. The marlin that kills a fish may not be the one that eats it, so cooperation between the members of the hunting party has to be very good indeed.

Humpback whales hunt cooperatively using a most

Left: Bluefin tuna are voracious, fast-swimming, warm-blooded predators that hunt in packs and migrate thousands of miles between feeding and breeding grounds. Below: A striped marlin pursues a ball of bait fish. Marlin often hunt cooperatively. With several marlin circling the school and taking turns feeding, the bait fish have no chance to escape.

remarkable technique. One or more whales submerge simultaneously and circle a school of herring or other small fish or krill (small shrimplike organisms). As they swim, the whales exhale bubbles that rise to the surface in shimmering curtains. The fish flee to the center of the circle, away from the reflective, noisy bubbles. The whales continue to circle, but they spiral inward as they continue to blow bubbles, drawing their "net" ever tighter around their prey.

When the food is dense enough, all the whales in the group charge upward through the center of the bubble net with their mouths open. The whales burst through the surface of the water with their flexible, pleated throats bulging to grotesque proportions with the tons of water and fish they have just engulfed. The water is squeezed out through the screens of fibrous baleen that hang down on each side of the whales' mouths, trapping the fish inside. The great tongues then wipe the fish off the baleen and push them to the back of the throat to be swallowed.

131

Opposite: *A pod of humpback whales feed cooperatively on a school of herring. After concentrating the fish into a compact ball, the whales rush upward with their mouths open, engulfing thousands of fish at once.*

*This orca, pounding the water's sur-
face with its tail, may be herding
prey, or it may be sending a signal to
other orcas within hearing range.*

This method of bubble-net feeding is an incredibly efficient method of destroying a school of fish and requires precise coordination between the whales involved. They seem to achieve this with acoustic signals.

KILLER WHALES. Orcas, or killer whales, also hunt herring cooperatively. As with humpbacks, the hunts appear to be coordinated with whistlelike acoustic signals. Orcas in the fjords of Norway have been filmed corralling herring by using their white undersides the same way the humpbacks use bubbles. Circling the school of fish and flashing their reflective white bellies at them cause the fish to draw together into an ever tighter school. When the panicked fish are packed tightly enough, the orcas begin to stun them by snapping their tail flukes into the school. As the stunned fish drift downward, the orcas circle back and swallow them. Like marlins, the whales do a certain amount of sharing, such as taking turns killing and eating.

Orcas feed on a very wide variety of prey, including fish, squid, rays, sharks, sea turtles, penguins, dugongs, sea lions, dolphins, porpoises, and other whales. It appears, however, that different groups of orcas specialize in different menu items. Orcas in Norway are experts at herding herring. Orcas in New Guinea are frequently seen feeding on sharks and giant ocean sunfish. In British Columbia two distinct types of orcas have been identified. The residents, which are present year-round, feed almost exclusively on salmon. Transients, which pass through the area only at certain times, specialize in marine mammals—sea lions and porpoises. The resident orcas vocalize frequently, whereas the transients are much quieter—presumably to avoid alerting their keen-eared prey.

Transient orcas can be found in almost any part of the world's oceans. Working as a team, they are able to tackle just about anything that swims. They have been seen feeding on a whale shark—the largest fish in the ocean—and on blue whales, the largest animals on the planet. When attacking a large whale,

Why They're Called "Killer" Whales

One group of orcas off the coast of Argentina specializes in hunting sea lions and elephant seals. They have developed a unique hunting method taught by one orca to another. Taking advantage of a deep channel that allows access to the beach on certain tides, they fling their ten-ton bodies out of the water and onto the beach in front of a sea lion colony. Seizing a baby sea lion, they wait for the next wave to lift them up so they can return to the sea. Sometimes two whales trap a pup between them so that it can't escape. The captured pup is sometimes used for training a young orca in hunting techniques before it is killed and eaten, much as a cat uses a mouse to teach her kittens to hunt. Sometimes the orcas seem merely to be playing with their food. They can repeatedly bat a helpless sea lion pup into the air with their tails or toss it into the air with their teeth.

Orca with sea lion pup

some orcas seize the fins to hamper the whale's swimming. Others swim on top of the whale's head to prevent it from rising up to take a breath. Others bite pieces out of the whale to sever its swimming muscles or cause it to bleed to death. The orcas take turns at these jobs so that they can come to the surface to breathe. When the whale has been disabled, the orcas eat what they want and leave the rest. Sometimes only the tongue is eaten.

HUMAN PARTNERS.
An extraordinary partnership developed between an orca and human whalers in Australia. For years the orca followed the whaling ships to sea. When a whale was harpooned, the orca would seize the harpoon line

Bottlenose dolphins feed primarily on fish. In some areas of the world, they have learned to cooperate with human fishermen to increase their catches.

in its teeth and help to subdue the whale. After the whale was brought back to the ship, the grateful whalers would cut out the whale's tongue and toss it to the waiting orca. When the orca finally died, its carcass was brought ashore and the skull enshrined in a museum. The grooves worn into the orca's teeth by holding harpoon lines can still be seen.

Bottlenose dolphins, smaller relatives of the orca, also sometimes work in partnership with humans. In such diverse parts of the world as South America and New Guinea, alliances have been formed between fishermen and dolphins that go back for generations. The dolphins herd a school of fish into the fishermen's nets. By trapping the fish against this barrier, they are able to catch fish more easily than they could by themselves. The humans are also able to take more fish with less effort.

Another species of dolphin, the spinner, cooperates with fishermen in Indonesia. The fishermen drop baited hooks from their canoes and wait. The dolphins herd yellowfin tuna toward the fishing lines, where they sometimes take a hook. The tuna, weighing up to 50 pounds each, are too big for the dolphin to catch or swallow, but the fishermen keep a supply of small mackerel to toss to the dolphins as a reward.

COOPERATION. In the eastern Pacific, it is the dolphin and tuna that work as partners. Both spinner and spotted dolphins are frequently seen swimming above schools of large yellowfin tuna. Just who is following whom is a subject of some

Atlantic spotted dolphins feed on squid and fish in deep offshore waters during the night. By day they move into shallower water to rest and play, sometimes snacking on flying fish or on wrasses buried in the sand.

Below: *Common dolphins move in large herds and feed cooperatively. Working together, they can surround a school of fish and completely eliminate it in a matter of minutes.*
Opposite: *Dolphins and pelicans feed together on a school of small fish.*

debate, but apparently both tuna and dolphin benefit by feeding together on schools of smaller fish. The tuna may assist the dolphin by driving the fish up when they attempt to escape by diving. The dolphins may help the tuna locate fish schools with their advanced sensory perception (see Chapter 5, "Secret Senses"). Tuna boats have learned to take advantage of this relationship by dropping nets around the dolphins, which are released later, in order to catch the tuna. The fishermen's observations, however, only add to the mystery of the dolphin-tuna relationship. They say that the tuna pass first, with the dolphins behind. However, when they use speedboats to herd the dolphins into a tight pack, the tuna stay underneath. Who is following whom?

Tunas, dolphins, and sharks all work in partnership with seabirds. The birds attack schools of fish from above, confusing them and driving them down, while the sea animals attack the fish from below, concentrating them and driving them up. Sometimes great feeding frenzies develop in the open ocean, when the water seems to boil as a

Dive Deep—Dive Hot

To take advantage of great shoals of squid, fish, and sea jellies found in deep water, air-breathing predators have developed astounding deep-diving capabilities. Elephant seals commonly dive to 1,000 feet to feed and have been tracked to depths of 5,200 feet. They can stay down for up to an hour and a half at a time, yet they rarely spend more than four minutes on the surface. While at sea they spend up to 90 percent of their time underwater. Biologists believe that they sleep on the way down to conserve oxygen. Sperm whales have been tracked to 3,900 feet confirmed and 6,600 feet estimated, but indirect evidence suggests they go much deeper. Whales caught at the surface in water 10,000 feet deep had fresh bottom-dwelling sharks in their stomachs.

Sperm whale

When scientists put a depth recorder on a leatherback turtle, it promptly dived to more than 4,000 feet—past the limit of the recorder. To find high concentrations of sea jellies to feed on, the turtles migrate more than 3,000 miles from their tropical nesting beaches to high latitudes where the sea temperature may be only 10 degrees Fahrenheit above freezing. All other reptiles become inactive at such low temperatures, but the leatherback remains active by raising its body temperature as much as 32 degrees Fahrenheit above the ambient temperature. Recent discoveries show that other supposedly cold-blooded creatures, including mako, porbeagle, white sharks, tuna, and marlin, all increase their hunting efficiency by maintaining body temperatures significantly higher than the water temperature. Marlins have a special heater organ that can warm them up to 45 degrees Fahrenheit above the ambient temperature.

school of fish is simultaneously attacked by several kinds of larger fish, sharks, birds, and dolphins or whales.

SOUND WAVES. The method dolphins use to actually capture their food is also a topic of some mystery. They are so extraordinarily successful at fishing that it sometimes seems as though they have some sort of secret weapon. Observers have seen apparently uninjured fish floating in helpless disorientation close to where dolphins have been feeding. And loud buzzing noises have been heard emanating from feeding dolphins—much louder than the noises they make when they are not feeding. It has been proposed that dolphins can send out "death beams" of noise so intense that they stun any fish in their path.

Some scientists believe that sperm whales also use sound to kill or disable their prey. According to this "big bang theory," the giant oil-filled forehead of the sperm whale is used to focus a crippling blast of sound at the fish and squid the whale feeds on. Others believe that the head is primarily a buoyancy-control organ. Allowing seawater to cool it could cause the oil to solidify into fat and

A bottlenose dolphin cruises across a sandy bottom. Using their echolocation, or sonar, capability, dolphins may find fish buried in the sand and dig them out.

The giant forehead of the sperm whale is filled with oil, which may be used to focus sound or as a buoyancy-control feature.

make the animal sink. At the bottom, the whale could divert warm blood to the head, liquefying the oil and making the whale buoyant enough to rise up without swimming. Control of buoyancy could be an important asset for an animal that dives more than a mile deep.

Regardless of the function of the oil in the head, sperm whales undoubtedly produce loud clicks when they are diving. At times these clicks become much

louder or more rapid than usual. Could it be that the whales are blasting their prey into submission with high-energy bursts of sound? The theory is very controversial.

A sperm whale calf, too young to feed on its own, waits near the surface while its mother dives deep for squid. Remoras are able to colonize its body since it cannot yet dive beyond the depths that they can endure.

UNEXPLAINED THEORIES. But the way sperm whales feed is curious in many ways. For one, in most individuals the teeth in the upper jaw never erupt, remaining buried in the gums throughout the animal's life. The teeth in the lower jaw do not erupt until years after the whale has been weaned and has been catching its own food. One captured adult whale had jaws broken so badly that the lower jaw stuck out at a 90-degree angle from the head. It was an old injury, and

yet the animal's stomach was full of squid. The stomach contents of even uninjured whales with a full set of teeth usually consist of whole squid and fish, without tooth marks, and sometimes still alive! Apparently sperm whales don't need their teeth, or perhaps even their lower jaws, to feed.

The lower jaw is extremely narrow in relation to the head and is set well back on the underside of the head. It would seem to be barely functional. And yet an adult male sperm whale is estimated to consume one and a half tons of food per day. The coloration of the lower jaw is curious as well. While the rest of the whale is dark gray or brown, the skin around the lower jaw and the lining of the mouth is brilliant white. It's possible that the whales need only to swim with their mouths open. The whale's passage could agitate bioluminescent organisms whose light may reflect off the white mouth lining and attract squid and fish right into the mouth. Sperm whales may possibly swim upside down while hunting to silhouette their prey against the dim light coming down from the surface.

It may be that sperm whales are simple suction feeders, vacuuming up shoals of curious or slow-moving squid. But how does that explain the large, fast-swimming fish, such as sharks and barracuda, that are sometimes found in their stomachs? And although most of the squid taken are small in relation to the whale—one to two feet long—sperm whales sometimes feed on giant squid. These monsters of the deep may weigh up to a thousand pounds and reach

Aquatic Archers

One of the most unusual adaptations for hunting found in the underwater world belongs to the archerfish, found in coastal swamps in the Indo-Pacific region. Because these fish can live in water ranging from salt to fresh, they have free passage up brackish tidal creeks where branches of mangrove trees hang low over the water. An archerfish can close its tongue around a groove running down the center of the roof of its mouth to form a tube that works like a blowgun. By suddenly clapping its gill covers shut, it can squirt water through the tube and out of its mouth. The archerfish aims rapid-fire bursts of water droplets at insects on the vegetation overhanging the creek. It can hit an insect and wash it into the water from up to ten feet away.

Archerfish

This remarkable feat is made possible partly by the anatomy of the archerfish's head. Most adult fish have their eyes on the sides, with each one working independently to give them almost 360-degree vision. But archerfish have both eyes facing forward, giving them stereoscopic vision, which allows them to judge distance. Their vision does not correct for refraction, which bends the light rays coming from the insect as they pass from air into water. The archerfish must learn from experience to make this correction rather than aiming directly at the image of the insect.

143

Opposite: *A sperm whale calf, accompanied by remoras, rests near the surface. The white lining of the mouth may serve to reflect bioluminescence in the deep waters where sperm whales feed.*

lengths of 60 feet—barely shorter than a fully grown male sperm whale. Large scars left by the suckers of enormous squid on the heads of some whales attest to the resistance a giant squid can put up when attacked. How does a whale subdue such an awesome adversary? And what to make of the headless octopuses that are sometimes found floating where sperm whales have been feeding? The "big bang theory" is no more improbable than any other concept to explain how sperm whales get their food.

One group of marine animals are definitely known to use stunning sound to capture their prey. Snapping shrimp, also known as pistol shrimp, have one enormously enlarged claw. The claw is locked open under tension by a latch mechanism. When the claw is held out to a passing fish or shrimp and the latch released, the claw pops shut with a bang that renders the prey helpless. The snap of a pistol shrimp's claw shutting can be heard half a mile away.

TOOL AND DIVE SPECIALISTS. Sea

otters are the only mammals apart from primates known to use tools to help them feed. A sea otter brings up a large, flat stone from the bottom, places it on its chest while floating belly-up at the surface, and bangs

Opposite: Most animals consume their food right where they find it. But sea otters bring shellfish from the seafloor up to the surface, where they can crack the shells open against a rock held on the stomach while floating.

Horn sharks feed principally on sea urchins, crabs, and other shellfish. Their broad, strong jaws with short teeth are well suited for crushing shellfish.

shellfish against it to crack open the shells. Otters feed mainly on sea urchins, crabs, clams, and abalone. Their penchant for commercially valuable shellfish, such as abalone, has led them into conflict with some commercial fishermen, who resent the protection otters have received under the Marine Mammal Act.

JAWS—MYTH AND REALITY.

The popular image of sharks—swimming around with jaws agape, devouring anything that crosses their paths—does faint justice to the striking diversity of diets and feeding methods found in this group of nearly 400 species of fish. The two species of the largest sharks, whale sharks and basking sharks, are both filter-feeders. They do swim around with gaping mouths, but only for the purpose of straining small fish and crustaceans out of the water.

Whale sharks sometimes ingest larger fish, up to the size of tunas. Some experts believe that these are swallowed accidentally when the tuna are feeding upon the same schooling fish as the whale sharks. In their frenzy, the tuna may chase the bait fish right into the shark's mouth. But some observers have described what appears to be a deliberate ruse by the whale shark. The shark stops swimming and orients itself in a vertical position, just beneath the bait school. It rises up slowly, mouth wide open. The bait fish seek shelter in what appears to them to be a large, dark cave. The larger fish swim inside to pursue the bait fish. The whale shark continues to rise upward until its head lifts above the water, and gravity carries the fish—big and small—down its throat.

Horn sharks, including the Port Jackson shark, are slow-moving, bottom-dwelling sharks that feed mostly upon invertebrates, including sea urchins, sea stars, worms, snails, crabs, shrimp, and barnacles. Their jaws, with flattened tooth plates for crushing the shells of their prey, are well adapted to their diet of shellfish.

Nurse sharks have a varied diet, including lobsters, crabs, and other shellfish, but also octopus and fish. Their strong jaws with short, sharp teeth are

A nurse shark feeds on a spiny lobster. The powerful jaws of the nurse shark are capable of producing a suction that can pull a prey animal from its hiding place in the reef.

adapted both for crushing hard-shelled prey and seizing softer-bodied animals. Like horn sharks, they feed mainly on the bottom, using suction to extricate their prey from hiding places.

Sand tiger sharks have long, needlelike teeth, perfectly suited for seizing slippery fish and squid in midwater. They also feed on small sharks, rays, crabs, and lobster. The prey is normally eaten whole. The narrow teeth are designed for seizing and holding fish, not for cutting them up.

Mako sharks start life with teeth similar to those of sand tigers, indicating that they are living on a similar diet, swallowing fish and squid whole. However, when makos reach a larger size, their teeth become broad and flat with sharp, serrated edges, like those of the great white shark. Not surprisingly, this change in tooth shape corresponds to a change in diet to larger fish such as swordfish and sometimes dolphins and turtles, which the mako saws into edible chunks with its built-in cutlery.

The great white shark's flat, triangular teeth are clearly designed to saw large chunks out of its prey. Small whites are believed to feed largely on fish, such as tuna, and have more narrow teeth than adults. Larger individuals have a varied diet but are believed to favor marine mammals, such as elephant seals and sea lions. These clever, warm-bodied creatures are fast and maneuverable. The

Above: *The spiky, backward-pointing teeth of the sand tiger shark are designed to seize and hold whole fish. The dark spots on the snout are sensory organs that detect electric fields.* Opposite: *The large, shearing teeth of the great white shark and its natural tendency to take large prey make it a threat to humans.*

Scalloped hammerhead sharks feed mostly at night, on deep-dwelling fish and squid. During the day they often school in shallower water.

white shark's only chance of taking a healthy individual is by surprise. Apparently whites often target their prey by swimming low and watching for silhouettes against the bright light of the surface.

Many attacks on humans by great white sharks are believed to be cases of mistaken identity resulting, for example, from a person on a surfboard resembling a sea lion when viewed in silhouette. In most cases the victim is spit out after the initial bite. This may be because the shark realizes it has seized something with a much lower fat—and energy—content than its intended prey. Or it may be part of the shark's normal feeding behavior to avoid injury from the struggling prey by allowing it to bleed to death before eating it. Regardless, the low total number of attacks on humans makes it clear that we do not constitute part of the normal diet of this or any other fish.

The great hammerhead shark uses its short, sharp, deeply serrated teeth to take a variety of prey, including fish, other sharks, squid, and crabs. One 15-foot great hammerhead caught by a fisherman was found to have a nine-foot lemon shark in its stomach. The hammerhead's preferred diet, however, appears to be rays. Hammerheads seem to be oblivious of the barbed venomous stingers some rays defend themselves with. Humans who have been pierced by one of these describe the pain as excruciating, and they have found that these wounds often result in tissue necrosis and a serious infection. Yet hammerhead sharks continue to feed with dozens of these stingers stuck in their mouths and throats.

Swimming Garbage Cans

The unusual curved, notched, and serrated teeth of the tiger shark seem to be particularly effective for sawing apart the shells of sea turtles—one of its favorite food items. However, tiger sharks have an extremely broad diet. They are both predators and scavengers. Their normal diet includes birds, fish, dolphins, sea snakes, invertebrates, and carrion. Human body parts are sometimes found in their stomachs. While tiger sharks occasionally attack live people, most of these parts likely result from their job of cleaning dead stuff out of the ocean. Probably the most indiscriminate feeders of all sharks, tiger sharks have yielded up such items as a suit of armor, a keg of nails, a roll of tar paper, a pair of tennis shoes, license plates, deer antlers, tin cans, reindeer, ducks, and a raincoat. Tiger sharks seem to have earned their reputation of "swimming garbage cans."

FEEDING UTENSILS.

Mammals have the upper jaw fused to the skull and the lower jaw hinged to it. But in most sharks, both jaws are only loosely attached to the skull. When they feed, the jaws can be thrown forward to seize a fish or

A large group of Caribbean reef sharks has been attracted by bait. This fish-eating species can be dangerous in uncontrolled situations but adapts quickly to controlled feedings and can be observed at close range with little hazard.

The whitetip reef shark feeds primarily by night, specializing in extracting fish, octopus, crabs, and lobsters from their hiding places in the coral reef. If a group of whitetip sharks is excited by a wounded fish hiding in the reef, they may actually break apart the coral to reach it.

to grasp a larger prey. If the prey is too large to be swallowed in one piece, the shark may shake its head back and forth until the teeth saw through the prey to remove a bite-size piece. People once thought that because a shark's mouth is on the underside of the head, it had to roll over to bite something at the water's surface. That was before people realized that a shark can throw its jaws right out in front of its nose.

A shark may break or lose a number of teeth when it attacks prey or if it seizes a female for mating. Since teeth are essential for the survival of a shark, they must be replaced. Most sharks have several rows of replacement teeth folded down just behind the functional teeth. When a tooth is lost, another is erected to take its place so that the shark can continue to feed efficiently. On average, a shark's teeth are replaced every two to three weeks. It can go through thousands in its lifetime.

Saw sharks and sawfish (a type of ray) have the most unusual and specialized teeth in this group of animals. They are mounted on either side of a long, flat bill that the animal uses as a broadsword. One kind of sawfish can grow up to 24 feet long with a six-foot bill. Charging through a school of fish, slashing its bill

A protective membrane comes up from beneath to shield the eye of a blue shark as it bites down on a mackerel. The electrical sense is more important than vision in the final moments of an attack, so many sharks cover their eyes to prevent injury by struggling prey.

from side to side, a sawfish can kill, injure, or dismember a number of fish. It then circles back to eat them.

Even more unusual is the feeding method of thresher sharks. The upper part of their tail fin is as long as the rest of the body. They swim through schools of fish cracking their tails like whips to stun and kill the fish. When they are caught on fishing lines, the hook is sometimes in the tail rather than the mouth.

Some sharks feed extensively on smaller sharks, and these may include members of their own species. But cannibalism is not limited to sharks. Many other creatures, including lobsters, crabs, octopuses, and skipjack tuna, are not averse to eating their own kind. Some fish, such as anchovies, eat the eggs of their own species. This may be an important way of regulating the size of the population so that it does not outstrip the food supply.

Above: *The sawfish has its teeth mounted along the edges of its long bill. It slashes through a school of fish, then circles back to eat the injured ones.* Opposite: *Although the long-nosed butterflyfish eats a variety of prey, it specializes in nibbling off the tube feet, tentacles, and other parts of sea urchins.*

154

SPECIALIZED TOOLS. Just as the teeth of sharks reflect their feeding habits, the mouths of butterflyfishes and the closely related angelfishes also reflect their highly specialized feeding habits. The elongated snout of the long-nose butterflyfish enables it to reach in between the spines of sea urchins to nibble their tube

feet. The much shorter snout of the pyramid butterflyfish is perfect for picking plankton out of midwater. The medium-length snout of the lined butterflyfish is well suited for picking at coral polyps.

The black-spot angelfish's tiny mouth is adapted to its diet of floating plankton. French, queen, and emperor angelfishes have larger, heavier jaws for tearing apart the sponges that form the bulk of their diet. Angelfishes are among the very few animals in the ocean able to feed on sponges. Most sponges are pro-

A French angelfish bites into an orange sponge. The bright orange color is a warning signal that the sponge is protected by toxic chemicals and needlelike spicules. Coating its food with mucus may help protect the angelfish.

tected by a variety of toxic compounds as well as needlelike spicules of silica, which protect them from predation by most fish. Coating their food with large quantities of mucus helps the angelfish avoid injury from the little glassy slivers of silica.

Some trunkfishes also feed on sponges. But most feed primarily on small bottom-dwelling invertebrates such as worms. The odd-looking mouth of the trunkfish, which always appears as if it is puckering up for a kiss, is serviceable for a most unusual hunting method. The trunkfish turns vertically, as though standing on its head, above a sand bottom. It directs a powerful jet of water through its puckered mouth into the sand, blasting out any little creatures that might be hiding there in the sediments on the seafloor.

Triggerfish also are capable of using water jets for feeding. Their favorite food is spiny sea urchins. Their eyes are protected from the spines of the urchins by being set extremely far back on the head—contributing to the triggerfish's comical appearance. Their lips are often "tattooed" purple by urchin spines.

Trunkfish use their puckered-up mouths to direct jets of water into the seafloor, blasting out small animals. This golden trunkfish is accompanied by a small wrasse, which hopes to share the food dislodged by the trunkfish.

Sometimes a queen triggerfish will direct a jet of water at the base of an urchin, flipping it over so that the fish can attack its unprotected underside.

The cartoonish mouths on the undersides of stingrays and eagle rays are used in a reverse fashion. Having detected a clam or other morsel buried under the sand, they lie flat on the sand and suck until they have vacuumed the prey item right out of the bottom.

Sharks are not the only fish that can sling their jaws out in front of them to seize prey. In fact, many fish can do this. But the champion of this trick is the sling-jaw wrasse. Its jaws can be extended up to a third of its body length in front

Opposite: *A triggerfish blasts the bottom with a jet of water, stirring up a cloud of sediments.* Below: *A yellow stingray rests on the seafloor, camouflaged by sand that it has shuffled on top of its body. The mouth and gills are hidden on the underside of the body.*

159

of the head, all in the flash of an eye. With its jaws extended, it looks as though it is feeding through a soda straw.

A DIET OF WATER.

Like angelfishes, leatherback turtles feed almost exclusively on a single food group—in this case, sea jellies. In order to find enough of these animals to sustain them, leatherbacks may migrate more than 3,000 miles from their breeding grounds in the tropics to cold temperate waters and then dive more than 3,000 feet down. Leatherbacks—at least the young ones small enough to be kept in a lab—can consume up to two times their body weight in jellyfish each day. Still, it is a mystery how they sustain themselves on this diet, since sea jellies consist almost entirely of water. Scientists studying this question burned jellyfish in a calorimeter to determine the en-

A loggerhead sea turtle attacks a queen conch. This turtle was unable to break the heavy shell, but a larger turtle would be able to crush it.

A loggerhead turtle eats a spiny lobster. Loggerheads are so fond of these that they have been known to take apart wooden lobster traps to get at the lobsters inside.

ergy content. It was so close to zero that in theory more energy is spent digesting one than could be obtained from it. Somehow, though, the turtles manage to derive enough calories from these watery creatures, not only to survive, but to grow to nearly ten feet in length and over a thousand pounds.

Loggerhead and ridley turtles consume a more varied diet including crabs, shrimp, clams, mussels, snails, tunicates, sea urchins, sea jellies, and other seden-

A Diet of Glass

Hawksbill turtles, along with certain angelfishes, filefishes, and nudibranchs (sea slugs), are among the few animals able to overcome the formidable defense systems of sponges and feed on them. Sponges are simple bottom-dwelling, filter-feeding animals that form a large part of many reefs. They have no outer skeleton or shell to protect them, and if approached by a predator, they can neither run away nor fight back. Instead they have evolved internal skeletal structures and an array of noxious and toxic chemical substances.

In some types of sponges, the skeletal structures are mostly composed of various types of tough fibers. Other kinds of sponges contain silica spicules—needlelike structures made up of the crystalline substance glass is made from. For unknown reasons, hawksbill turtles specialize in feeding on the very types of sponges highest in silica, which is completely indigestible. In some turtles examined by biologists, silica made up more than half of the weight of the gut contents—more than a pound of raw glass! One researcher, after finding that these sponges comprised around 95 percent of the food in the digestive tracts of the turtles she examined, concluded that hawksbills live on "a diet of glass."

Some of the hawksbills' favorite sponges also contain chemicals toxic enough to kill fish and other kinds of turtles. How hawksbills protect themselves against these substances is not known, but sometimes enough is absorbed into their bodies to make the flesh of the turtles toxic.

tary or slow-moving prey. The loggerhead, with its massive beak, is said to be one of only two creatures in the ocean capable of crushing the thick shell of an adult queen conch. The other is the eagle ray.

GRAZERS. When newly hatched, green turtles will eat almost anything that comes across their path. However, as they mature they switch to a predominately vegetarian diet, consisting mostly of sea grasses and algae. One of the reasons green turtles bask in the sun may be that their vegetarian fare does not supply them with sufficient vitamin D.

Dugongs and manatees, aptly known as "sea cows," are also grazers. They evolved independently from the other marine mammals, which are carnivorous. Their closest relatives are elephants. Their bulbous snouts look almost like very short trunks and are used much like the trunks of elephants—to pass food to the mouth. They do not bite off the sea grasses but use their flexible prehensile lips to grasp and tear them free. The grasses are then passed back into the

mouth, where they are crushed by a horny mouth pad and flattened molars in the back of the mouth.

The teeth of manatees are replaced on an assembly-line basis, with the teeth moving from back to front as the ones in the front are worn out. Only one other species of animal in the world has this system of tooth replacement—a type of kangaroo. In addition to sea grasses, manatees feed on tree leaves that have

Opposite: A green sea turtle feeds on algae growing on the reef. As adults, green turtles have a predominantly vegetarian diet. Above: Here a manatee is feeding on sea grasses. Manatees spend six to eight hours a day feeding.

fallen into the water and on floating vegetation such as water hyacinths. Like cows and horses, manatees and dugongs can't finish digesting their food without the help of symbiotic bacteria to break down the cellulose. To accommodate this slow process, which can take up to a week, manatees and dugongs have extremely long digestive tracts. The intestine of a dugong can be more than 80 feet long!

Spiny sea urchins are also grazers. During the day long-spined black sea urchins tend to remain stationary in holes in the reef, looking like simple pincush-

Opposite: *A Florida manatee enters a freshwater spring. When the weather is warm the manatees move out into estuaries or the ocean to feed on sea grasses and other vegetation. During cold spells they seek shelter in the warm springs.* Left: *A purple sea urchin feeds on a giant kelp plant. If the urchin eats all the way through the kelp at the base, the entire upper part of the plant will drift away. Whole forests of kelp have been destroyed in this way when sea urchin populations exploded.*

Sea urchins are grazers. The complex jaws on the underside are used to scrape algae off the reef or seafloor. The round shell is the empty skeleton of a dead sea urchin.

ions. But by night they scuttle about the reef, scouring off the coating of algae that has grown during the day. They also graze down the sea grasses just next to the reef, creating a halo around the reef.

The mouth of the sea urchin is one of the most complex feeding structures in the animal kingdom. It is known to biology students as "Aristotle's lantern," for the Greek scientist and philosopher who first described its intricate structure as resembling a lantern. These prickly relatives of the sea star were greatly underappreciated (especially by divers who bumped into them) until a mysterious plague in the early 1980s wiped out most of the urchins in the West Indies. Without these much-maligned "street sweepers" to keep the reefs clean, many of the reefs in the area were overgrown by algae, which began to smother the coral.

In California, on the other hand, the overhunting of sea otters, which feed on urchins, caused the urchins to proliferate. They became a menace to kelp, destroying whole forests of the giant algae by nibbling off the holdfasts attaching the kelp to the bottom. The problem was resolved when it was discovered that the Japanese would pay very high prices for fresh sea urchin roe, which they eat raw. A booming industry in urchin collecting resulted. The sea otters are also making a comeback under protection.

A number of fish, including most species of parrotfish and surgeonfish, are also herbivores. Parrotfish are often seen scraping the reef with their large, hard

A parrotfish scrapes algae from the surface of a dead coral with its beaklike fused teeth. Some of the coral skeleton is ingested along with the algae and will be ground into fine sand and excreted.

"Plantimals"

Lettuce-back sea slugs feed primarily on algae, but they do not digest all of what they eat. The algae's chloroplasts (the green cell parts that carry on the process of photosynthesis) are not digested but transferred intact to the ruffles on the back of the slug. Like many other sea slugs, these have developed elaborate skin ruffles on the back to absorb oxygen from the seawater, functioning as secondary gills. But in this species the ruffles also become organs of photosynthesis, exposing the borrowed chloroplasts to sunlight to produce food. The lettuce-back sea slug is then part plant, part animal. They are aptly named, because their frilly green backs give them the appearance of a crawling salad. Other marine animals, including some corals, clams, and sponges, perform a similar trick by hosting live algae within their tissues.

Lettuce-back sea slug

beaks. However, very few kinds of parrotfish feed on live corals. More commonly they scrape algae off the surface of dead corals. In the process they remove some of the limestone skeleton of the coral. This is crushed by the grinding plates in the fish's throat and passed through the gut along with the algae.

Some kinds of algae produce their own limestone skeletons, which are also ground up and passed through the guts of parrotfish that eat them. After the nutrients are removed by the intestine, the crushed limestone is excreted by the parrotfish as fine, white sand. A single parrotfish can produce a considerable quantity of sand in a day. It is believed that much of the white sand around coral reefs and on beaches in the tropics is the result of feeding activity by parrotfish.

Some kinds of parrotfishes and other animals, such as green turtles and sea cows, feed mostly on sea grasses. Many encrusting organisms grow on the blades of sea grass, and others hide in sea grasses and in clumps of algae. These small animals may contribute significantly to the nutrition of the animals that feed on the grasses and algae, adding protein and other nutrients. Thus these herbivores, while not predatory, are not strictly vegetarian either.

FARMERS. Some herbivores do not graze the reef but cultivate their own gardens of algae. Certain damselfishes prefer specific kinds of algae. In order to promote the growth of their preferred variety, they first prepare an area for it to grow on. If a suitable patch of dead substrate is not available, they create one by nipping at the coral until they have killed it in that area. However, they never kill more than a small amount of the coral in the territory they defend. They also drive off other animals that might damage the coral. More live coral ends up in their territories than is found in areas not defended by damselfish. They also attack and destroy unwanted varieties of algae, leaving only a carefully tended lawn of the desired type. This garden patch is vigorously defended against any other fish that might try to poach it. The damselfish drives off fish many times larger than itself and may even attack divers. Spiny sea urchins may be picked up by one of the spines and bodily evicted from the territory. Surgeonfish, however, circumvent the damsels' defenses by attacking en masse. The damselfish can chase only one intruder at a time, so it is easily overcome by a swarm of surgeonfish descending on its territory in a hungry mob.

FILTER FEEDERS.

Many animals in the ocean do not find it necessary to grow their food, hunt for it, or even go out and graze it. Such an enormous amount of food is suspended in the water that billions of organisms thrive by merely sifting small plants, animals, and bits of detritus out of the passing currents. These include the beautiful, ornate little Christmas tree worms and their relatives,

sponges, feather stars or crinoids, sea fans and other gorgonians, clams, and tunicates or sea squirts. Porcelain crabs, which look as though they are waving Japanese fans when they feed, are also in this group, as

Above: A pair of Christmas tree worms feed side by side. Their feathery gill tufts sift plankton from the water. The slightest disturbance will cause the worm to retract its crown.
Left: Two porcelain crabs sift the water for plankton from the safety of their home under the stinging tentacles of a sea anemone. The white appendages near the mouth terminate in a "basket" of fine golden fibers, which is scooped through the water to filter out floating microorganisms.

are barnacles, which kick their "hairy" legs out of their shell and scoop them back toward their mouths.

The dominant filter feeders on West Indian reefs are sponges. These primitive animals are able to filter out particles as small as bacteria. Studies have shown that a sponge can remove up to 96 percent of the bacteria from the water that circulates through it. Collectively, the sponges on a West Indian reef remove most to nearly all the organic matter produced by that reef. They are a major factor in keeping the water clear around coral reefs.

Other animals do not wait for the current to bring food to them, but go out and actively filter it out of the water. The two largest fish in the ocean—whale sharks and basking sharks—are both filter feeders, as are most of the great whales, including right whales, sei whales, Bryde's whales, humpback whales, fin whales, minke whales, gray whales, and blue whales. Basking sharks and right whales merely swim slowly through the water with mouths open, filtering out minute plankton such as krill and copepods. A basking shark processes more than 2,000 cubic yards of water each hour, filtering out millions of these creatures, each less than an inch long. The others have a more varied diet, ranging from tiny plankton up to medium-size fish, and may pursue their food more actively.

The diet of fin whales, for example, includes krill, squid, capelin, sand lance, herring, and lanternfish. The fin whale is asymmetrical—the two sides of its body do not match. While the left side of its face is dark, like most of the body,

Behemoths of the Sea

Blue whales are not only the largest mammals in the sea—they are the largest animals that have ever lived on earth. They can reach over 100 feet in length and can weigh up to 160 tons. The heart can be as large as a compact car, and a person could crawl through the main artery leading out of it. It is ironic that the biggest creature on the planet feeds on some of the smallest. A blue whale is about 100 million times as large as the animals it eats.

Blue whales are fairly specialized in their diet, concentrating on the small shrimplike creatures known as krill. A feeding blue whale can consume up to eight tons of krill a day and may have more than a ton of krill in its stomach at one time. In order to find this food in sufficient concentration, blues must travel enormous distances. Recent underwater observations of blue whales have dispelled the image of a great bloated creature, slowly skimming through the water with its mouth open. Divers report that the whales appear very long and slender, with the head wider than the body. They dash like greyhounds from one patch of krill to another. Only upon reaching the krill does the massive mouth open. And only then does the pleated throat balloon out, taking in hundreds of gallons of water (about half the volume of its body), which is then forced out through the baleen plates, trapping the krill inside.

the lower right side is white. This may be related to its feeding behavior. When feeding on plankton, fin whales are simple surface skimmers. But one theory is that when feeding on schooling fish, the whale flashes the bright side of its head at the prey to frighten and concentrate them and turns with the dark left side toward them when it comes in to feed. Fin whales sometimes make loud popping noises when feeding. Some scientists believe these are produced in the jawbones

The basking shark feeds only on tiny planktonic organisms, which it obtains by swimming slowly through the water with its enormous mouth open. It swims at about two miles per hour while feeding.

The white feeding tentacles of a medusa worm extend out from the tube where the worm's body is hidden and across a red sponge dotted with commensal zoanthids. Periodically the worm withdraws the tentacles to feed on food particles that stick to them.

and frighten the prey toward the inside and back of the mouth to keep them from escaping from the mouth.

Gray whales feed occasionally on the surface or in midwater, like other whales, but more often on the bottom. They pump up sediments through one side of the mouth and filter out small shrimplike creatures, worms, and shells.

STICKY SITUATIONS. Some animals feed on small particles but without using filters. They use the "flypaper method," which seems to be equally effective. What looks like a mass of spaghetti noodles extending out from a small hole in the reef most likely belongs to a medusa worm, which has its segmented body hidden in an underground tube. The long, sticky tendrils are extended out and collect food particles that adhere to them. Periodically the tentacles are drawn in and are passed across the mouth for feeding.

Comb jellies look like jellyfish, but they have no stinging cells. Instead, they have sticky cells on their feeding tentacles. Like the medusa worms, they pull the tentacles

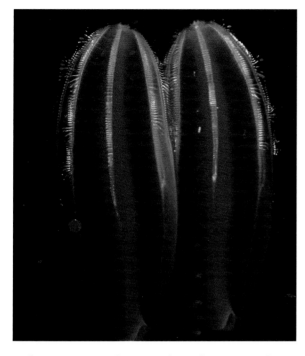

up and across the mouth to slurp off whatever food has attached to them. One type lacks tentacles and feeds on other comb jellies, swallowing them whole.

MUD SUCKERS. Food particles tend to pile up on the bottom, providing a nearly endless and readily accessible food supply for those animals equipped to take advantage of it. Some sea cucumbers plow along the bottom taking bottom sediments into the mouth and passing them out the other end, after absorbing the nutrients in the detritus. Their bodies can almost be thought of as open tubes, just passing around part of the seafloor as they scavenge. Mullet fish are more active bottom feeders. They take in mouthfuls of bottom sediments and sort them within the mouth. All the particles that are too large or too small are spit back out. The particles of the preferred size are passed through the gut, and the nutrients are absorbed. Theirs would be an easy life were it not for the many larger fish that prey on mullet.

Left: Comb jellies, also known as sea walnuts or by the scientific name ctenophores, look like stinging jellies, but most species have no stinging cells. Instead the type shown here swallows its food whole upon contact. This type feeds on other comb jellies.
Below: Some sea cucumbers trap particles suspended in the water, but most feed on bottom deposits. Some merely plow through the sediments with their mouths open. Others, such as this one, use feeding tentacles to transfer particles into their mouths.

Survival Instincts

With hungry predators surrounding them in three dimensions, it is no wonder that marine creatures have evolved a wonderful variety of ways to avoid ending up in another animal's belly. Perhaps the most common strategy is to prevent themselves from being seen. The great majority of animals in the ocean are camouflaged in some way. This is especially true in the open ocean, where the option of dashing into a hiding place is not available. In this

1
7
5

A group of Atlantic spotted dolphins travel in close formation. By sticking together, dolphins are able to defend themselves against sharks and other predators, which could more easily pick off an individual traveling alone.

Above: *A Caribbean reef squid uses rapid color changes to confuse predators. It is also capable of ejecting a cloud of ink, which distracts and disorients the predator as well as briefly disguising the squid while it jets away quickly in an unexpected direction.* Right: *Squid are highly intelligent and social animals that are able to warn each other of approaching predators by changing the color patterns of their skin. The pattern can even identify the specific type of animal that is approaching.*

environment, most of the fish, as well as other animals including whales, dolphins, sea turtles, and penguins, have adopted a pattern of countershading. The upper surface of the animal is dark, to blend in with the dim ocean depths when viewed from above. And the underside is a light color, to match the bright surface of the ocean when viewed from below. Some deepwater fish, such as lantern fish, even have light organs on their bellies so they can generate enough light to perfectly match the light coming down from above. Certain kinds of African catfish swim upside down. To maintain the effectiveness of the countershading in that position, they have dark bellies and light backs instead of the reverse. Many squid, which control their color pattern

through their nervous systems, can instantly reverse the pattern when they flip over, in order to keep the upper part of their bodies dark and the lower part pale.

MASTERS OF MASQUERADE. Even the largest fish in the ocean, the whale shark, is countershaded. In addition, the backs of these slow-moving titans are speckled with white polka dots. This seems to be a form of disruptive coloration, breaking up the shape of the animal so its form is less visible. It may also help the shark blend in with the rays of sunlight penetrating the ocean in the surface waters where it usually swims. But is it really possible to hide a 60-foot fish in the open ocean? And what creature need these monsters hide from?

In spite of their impressive size and sandpapery hide, which can be up to six inches thick, scars and mutilations indicate that whale sharks do have enemies. They may be subject to attack by smaller predatory sharks. And at least one sighting has been confirmed of a whale shark being eaten by orcas (killer whales). In the undersea wilderness, even the biggest animals have to hide from the constant threat of sudden death.

Fish living in different habitats adopt different types of camouflage to blend in. The leafy sea dragon sports weedy appendages all over its body that make it indistinguishable from the fronds of kelp (large seaweed) that it lives in. Sea horses can change their color to match the plant, sponge, or coral that they

Roving Eyes

The flatfish called flounders are masters of camouflage. Lying flat on the bottom, they match its color and pattern so perfectly that they are practically invisible. Like sea horses and other fish, flounders can change their color by expanding or contracting sacs of pigment in their skin. In laboratory experiments they have been able to match an astounding variety of colors and patterns, including polka-dot and checkerboard patterns.

Juvenile flounders swim upright like other fish. As they mature, however, their bodies change in preparation for a bottom-dwelling existence. Most notably, one eye migrates around to the other side of the head, so that both eyes will be useful when the fish lies on its side. Flounders are divided into left-eyed and right-eyed families, depending upon which side the eyes end up on.

Peacock flounder

Below: *A pipefish contours its body to a branch of soft coral. The color of the pipefish also matches that of the soft coral.* Right: *The body of a leafy sea dragon is covered with weedlike fleshy extensions matching the seaweeds in which the fish hides.* Opposite: *The frills and projections on the decorated warbonnet are usually enough to disguise it effectively as a clump of seaweed. But the disguise has failed to deceive this lingcod, which is making a meal of the warbonnet.*

attach themselves to. One public aquarium had had a brown sea horse on display for a year before they added a red Santa Claus to its tank for a Christmas decoration. Within a week the sea horse turned bright red to match the new feature in its environment.

Some fish and shrimp use an absence of color to camouflage themselves. Small gobies and anemone shrimp, in particular, are sometimes completely transparent, except for their internal organs. Details of the reef behind them can be clearly seen right through their bodies. Other fish have reflective scales, which mirror the colors around them.

For some fish, shape is equally as important as color, or more so, as an essential element of camouflage. These include flattened fish such as flounder, halibut, goosefish, toadfish, and crocodile fish, and lumpy fish such as frogfish, sargassum fish, scorpionfish, clingfish, and lumpfish. Flattened fish are almost always found lying on the bottom. Lumpy fish may be lying on the bottom or clinging to something else. Long, skinny fish, such as pipefish, trumpetfish, cornetfish,

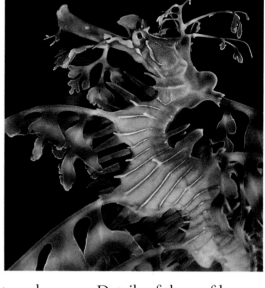

Its camouflage pattern, which both matches the background and breaks up the shape of the fish's body, renders the crocodile fish almost invisible as it lies on the reef.

and shrimpfish, are most likely to be found hovering next to a similarly shaped object, such as a thin-branched sponge, whip coral, blade of grass, or sea urchin spine. Needlefish and halfbeaks are exceptions. These long, slender, and silvery fish swim just under the surface of the ocean, blending in with the undersides of the waves.

PROTEAN CREATURES.

Octopuses and their cousins, cuttlefish and squid, are also doyens of deceit. Many have not only pigment cells, but also reflective cells in their skin. If they don't possess the right pigment color to match a background, they can use their reflective cells to pick up the color of whatever is around them.

Octopuses and cuttlefish can change not only the color, but also the shape and texture of their bodies, raising lumps on their skin to match a rough surface they are hiding on. An octopus can alter the size of its body as well. By spreading its arms apart and stretching a membrane between them in a "parachute" maneuver, it can suddenly increase its apparent size by several fold. It can also contract itself to an almost ropelike shape to squeeze through an opening the width of the distance between its eyes.

Octopuses can either crawl away from danger or shoot through the water under jet propulsion. By pointing the siphon through which they force the water that drives them, they can move in any direction. Under severe threat, they will discharge a cloud of ink, which both conceals their escape and provides a false target for the predator to attack.

A Caribbean reef octopus performs a "parachute" maneuver. In this case the maneuver is being performed defensively, but it can also be used to trap fish or crabs beneath the mantle for feeding.

A giant octopus jets away, streaming behind a cloud of ink. Some observers have reported that the ink cloud discharged by an octopus or squid can resemble the shape of the body of the animal that released it, fooling the predator into attacking the ink blob.

SMOKE SCREENS AND FLASHLIGHTS. Squid and cuttlefish also use jet propulsion and smoke screens of ink to escape predators. Squid sometimes darken themselves before expelling their ink, then blanch as they make their escape. Some kinds of deep-sea squid have luminous ink, which must provide quite a distraction as the squid bolts away in the darkness.

Some ostracods, tiny clamlike crustaceans, can also discharge liquid "flares" of luminous ink. When an ostracod is seized by a nocturnal predator, such as a cardinalfish, the fish may be so startled by the sudden flash of light in its mouth that it spits the ostracod back out unharmed. Sea hares emit a cloud of deep purple ink when disturbed. The ink both startles the predator and provides a warning to other nearby sea hares. They respond to ink in the water by retracting their heads or by fleeing.

Flashlight fish cultivate colonies of light-emitting bacteria in special organs under their eyes. Different kinds of flashlight fish have different methods for turning their headlights on and off. Some have eyelid-type shutters that cover the organs to block the light. Others can rotate them around to face the body when they don't want the light to be visible. On dark nights on the deep reef, or in caves in shallower water, these small fish can be seen blinking away like fireflies. When approached by a predator, they merely extinguish their lights and dash away in the darkness.

Sperm whales feed mostly on squid, which may account partly for the inky appearance of their liquid feces. Although large and powerful, sperm whales are subject to predation by orcas, pseudorcas or false killer whales, sharks, and humans. When frightened they sometimes defecate into

The light organ beneath the eye of a dark-bodied flashlight fish is used in both feeding and mating. When danger approaches, the light is turned off, and the fish scurries away.

Eight Arms to Drown You

Octopuses, the most intelligent invertebrates known, would rather run or hide than fight. But if seized by a predator, they can put up a formidable defense. They can deliver a venomous bite with their beak (adequate to kill a human, in the case of the blue-ringed octopus). However, they are more inclined to use their eight powerful sucker-studded arms to try to overcome their adversary.

Breath-holding divers who speared or grabbed a large octopus have narrowly escaped drowning when the octopus grabbed them back and held tight to the bottom with its other arms. Giant Pacific octopuses have been known to dislodge masks and yank away air hoses of scuba divers who molested them. There are even stories of octopus taking away a diver's speargun.

Researchers in Portugal discounted fishermen's stories of octopuses drowning dolphins until the researchers themselves witnessed an attack on a large octopus by a bottlenose dolphin. The dolphin came to the surface with the octopus in its mouth. But the octopus was able to reach around the dolphin's head and into the blowhole, the most sensitive part of a dolphin's anatomy. The dolphin then seemed to release the octopus, which crawled right up on top of the dolphin's head, obstructing its breathing. The dolphin became very distressed and began to leap about until it was able to knock off the octopus. The researchers saw dolphins feeding on cuttlefish on several occasions, but this was the only time they saw one try to take an octopus.

the water, creating a large inky cloud that conceals them as they dive into the depths. The fecal cloud is about the same color as the whales' bodies, so to a predator approaching from a distance, it may appear as though a group of whales is still there for some time after the whales have departed.

KUNG FU FLOWERS. Sperm whales sometimes form a collective defense pattern known as a "marguerite formation," because the whales arrange themselves like the petals of a marguerite flower. They are most likely to do this, rather than dive, if there are juveniles in the group. Though adult sperm whales can dive deeper than any of their predators, the young cannot escape attaining

A group of sperm whales begins a dive into the depths of the ocean to feed.

such great depths. The whales arrange themselves in a circle with the babies in the center and with their flukes pointing outward. In this way they are able to discourage predators with mighty blows from their powerful tails. The defense is usually successful.

Other marine animals band together for collective defense. Dolphins and sea lions are both known to gang up on sharks to drive them away from their young. Dolphins have been reported to even kill sharks on occasion, by attacking as a group and ramming them in the gills or other vital organs. Little anthias fish,

When a group of sperm whales is threatened, the whales arrange themselves with their heads together and their powerful tail flukes outward to repel attackers. Vulnerable calves are kept at the center. Because the whales are positioned like the petals of a flower, this is known as a marguerite, or lotus flower, formation.

or fairy basslets, ususally respond to danger by diving into the coral for cover. But they may surround a scorpionfish that has entered their territory, mobbing it almost like blue jays mobbing a cat. They are not able to harm the scorpionfish, but they can continually draw attention to it and deprive it of the element of surprise it needs for a successful attack. They may even be able to draw the attention of a larger predator that might threaten or drive off the scorpionfish.

The distress calls given off by some fish when they are injured are speculated to be a sort of last-ditch effort to attract a bigger predator, which might

Opposite: *Sea lions are social animals that cooperate to drive sharks away. When filmmakers put a remote camera by a sea lion colony, they were astonished to see sea lions following a great white shark. Apparently the shark can make a successful attack only if it can surprise the sea lions.*
Above: *Anthias fish, or fairy basslets, have been filmed apparently mobbing a scorpionfish.*

What's Scaring the Sharks?

Near certain islands and seamounts in the tropical eastern Pacific Ocean, schools of scalloped hammerhead sharks numbering into the hundreds patrol endlessly just off the edge of the reef. They are not searching for food. These animals feed individually at night in deep water. During the day they appear to be mostly just resting and waiting for the night. Why, then, do they school? Protection from predators is one of the main advantages for most schooling fish. What does an eight-foot shark have to be afraid of? That thought was even scarier to scuba divers than the idea of being surrounded by hundreds of sharks.

Noting that the schools are made up largely (but not entirely) of females, researchers proposed that they have a social function. Aggressive interactions occur between the sharks, and they compete for preferred positions near the center of the school. Mating has occasionally, but rarely,

Hammerhead sharks

been seen in these schools. It was suggested that they form a social hierarchy and that the males go to the center of the school to find a dominant female for a mate.

Scientists reasoned that the schools could not be defensive in nature because the sharks themselves are top predators. However, recent sightings of orcas feeding on hammerhead sharks may suggest reconsidering the possibility of a defensive function. Divers have also reported that the schooling sharks are extremely timid and flee from divers' bubble trails. So what is it that these sharks are so scared of?

attack the smaller predator attacking the injured fish. The distress call may also serve to warn other members of the school. An alarm may be given as a chemical signal as well as by a noise or a body signal. Some fish have special skin cells that release an alarm scent into the water when they are damaged. If water containing this scent is added to an aquarium containing fish of the same species, they react immediately by trying to flee or hide.

PRECISION CHOREOGRAPHY.

One of the most effective and widespread methods of collective defense is schooling. About half of all fishes spend at least part of their lives in a school, and a quarter school throughout their lives. While fish may aggregate with their own kind for feeding, reproduction, or social reasons, defense is certainly a primary reason for schooling.

In a school, as opposed to an aggregation, the fish are polarized—all pointing in the same direction. They are also evenly spaced, maintain the same position relative to the other fish, and swim at the same speed. A school does not necessarily consist of all the same kind of fish. Several different species may be mixed together. But it is important that they all look alike and be about the same size. And they all must be able to swim at the same speed. Therefore, fish can school with other similar-looking fish of the same size, but usually not with different age classes of their own species.

The great advantage of schooling is in preventing a predator from being able to target a single fish. Any fish that stands out from the group may end up dead. Interestingly, experiments have shown that although individual schooling fish such as minnows may be indistinguishable to predators or to humans, they do recognize each other as individuals, and they remember each other even after

A school of yellowtail grunts finds safety in numbers. Each individual's chance of becoming a meal for a larger fish is reduced by associating with other similar fish.

A school of silvery scad showers outward in response to the approach of a potential predator, the bottlenose dolphin. If the dolphin cannot isolate an individual fish to pursue, it cannot make a successful attack. Any fish that looks or acts differently from the rest becomes an easy meal.

being separated for periods of at least two months. Furthermore, schooling behavior is more efficient with fish that know each other.

By responding to a predator's rush with a coordinated movement of the entire school, the school can cause the predator to lose its focus on the fish it was chasing. In order to make a successful attack, the predator has to select a single target and follow it as it tries to escape. By just charging through a school of fish, even though there may be thousands of them, the predator will usually end up

with nothing. This phenomenon is well known to bird hunters, who learn to aim at a single bird rather than firing blindly into a flock. It is one of nature's most fascinating spectacles to watch a school of small fish "fountaining" around a predator such as a barracuda or tarpon. The larger fish charges into what seems to be a solid mass of bite-size snacks, only to find itself swimming through an empty tunnel with fish on all sides.

Schooling fish often enhance the effectiveness of these maneuvers with reflective scales. As they perform their evasive maneuvers, their silvery scales catch the sunlight, creating scintillating patterns that move in different directions from the movement of the fish, dazzling and confusing the predator. Most of the predator's strikes are unsuccessful. Usually a fish that ends up as a meal is injured or sick and unable to keep up with the movements of the school.

SAFETY IN NUMBERS.

How schooling fish coordinate the intricate choreography of their evasive patterns remains a mystery, but it is certain that the skills are instinctive and not learned. Vision seems to be important in maintaining schools, but other senses are required as well. Many schools break up at night.

A school of baitfish pulses and swirls around a coral reef. The motion and reflectivity of the fish create confusing patterns that make it almost impossible for a predator to pick out an individual fish.

192

Above: *Most schools of fish, such as this swarm of blue-lined snappers, consist of a single species. But different kinds of fish can school together if they are the same size and look very similar. Opposite: Stonefish are protected not only by an amazing camouflage, but also by highly venomous dorsal spines.*

The reason may be that the fish in the school can't see each other, but it may just as well be that the school is not needed in the absence of visual predators. Predators active at night use smell and vibration rather than sight to find their prey. These signals are magnified in a group, so it may actually be safer to be alone at night.

Defeating the attacks of some predators is not the only advantage of being a part of a school. A predator can eat only so many fish at a time. The more fish that surround an individual, the greater the chance that the victim will be somebody else. Each fish also benefits from the ability of the others to detect approaching predators. Even in a very large school, fish at the far side react to the approach of a predator almost simultaneously with those at the near side. And some schools can be very large. Schools of herring in the north Atlantic can contain up to 6 billion fish. When mullet migrate in the Caspian Sea, schools join together to form chains that can stretch for more than 60 miles.

STINGERS. Stonefish and scorpionfish masquerade very successfully as rocks on the bottom. Able to remain motionless almost indefinitely, and covered with fleshy flaps that look like algae, they are extremely difficult to differentiate from the bottom they rest on. But for the discerning predator able to penetrate their disguise, they have an additional surprise—venomous fin spines that can be

erected to provide a lethal deterrent. The venom of stonefish is powerful enough to kill a human in less than an hour, and it is said to be agonizing in its effect.

Underwater Rainbows

For the persistent predator not deterred by the camouflage or poison spines, some kinds of scorpionfish have a supplementary trick. While most of the scorpionfish's body is a drab brown (or shades of red, which appear brown in the blue light of the ocean), hidden on the underside of the pectoral fins is a brilliant rainbow pattern. If the scorpionfish is so threatened that it feels the need to flee, it spreads open its pectoral fins as it starts to swim, suddenly revealing the rainbow and startling the predator. It puts on a burst of speed, then abruptly folds the pectorals in and settles onto the reef, becoming once again nearly invisible in its camouflage.

This "startle coloration" is exactly the same trick employed by certain grasshoppers. When frightened into flight, they display a hidden red or yellow

Flying gurnard

pattern on their wings, which suddenly vanishes when they stop a short distance away and fold their wings. Flying gurnards are fish that look something like large grasshoppers. They are not able to fly, but they give the appearance of flying underwater when they spread their enormous winglike pectoral fins and swim. Normally they stay on the bottom and "walk" about slowly on their ventral fins, which they can even use like hands to turn over rocks and search for food. Their drab coloration enables them to blend in with the sand and rubble bottoms where they live. When threatened, they suddenly spread the pectoral "wings," displaying a brilliant pattern of iridescent blue to startle the predator, dash away, and close the "wings."

Injuries to humans usually happen when the victim steps on an unseen stonefish while wading. Even though most of the victims do survive, they suffer a great deal of pain and undergo some long-term tissue damage.

More than 200 species of marine fish are protected by venomous spines, including lionfish, catfish, ratfish, sea robins, goosefish, rabbitfish, toadfish, stargazers, spiny dogfish (a small shark), Port Jackson sharks, and saber squirrelfish. Rabbitfish have 24 poisoned spines in all. They are highly prized as food fish, but fishermen have learned to handle them with care.

Some sea urchins are protected by mildly toxic bristling spines covered with tiny reverse barbs. Once a spine penetrates the flesh of an attacker (or a clumsy diver), it continues to work its way into the body with each movement of the flesh around the spine. Some urchins are also protected by venomous pedicellariae—tiny sets of jaws in between the spines. These poison pinchers will not release a victim even after they have been torn loose from the urchin.

Bristle worms have very fine glasslike hollow spines, which are mildly venomous. They are erected whenever the worm is disturbed. In human skin they produce an irritation similar to that caused by fiberglass. Crown-of-thorns starfish are covered by venomous spines that help to protect them from predation by just about everything except triton trumpet snails, which eat them with relish. The spines can cause painful wounds in humans.

VENOMOUS BARBS.

Stingrays, eagle rays, and cow-nosed rays have spines at the base of the tail, which are used strictly for defense. The spines, like those of sea urchins, have reverse barbs that cause them to work forward with the muscular action of the body they penetrate. A dolphin stung while pestering a stingray can have the barb remain in its

Left: In contrast to other venomous fish, which have only a few dangerous spines, rabbitfish, such as this fox-face rabbitfish, have venomous spines in all, or most, of the fins on their body. Below: The purple sponge uses noxious chemicals to make itself distasteful to predators, while the sea urchin relies on its hard spines to make itself unpalatable.

The brittle glasslike spines of bristle worms, or fire worms, break off in the skin or flesh of any animal that touches them. The mildly venomous spines can cause a skin irritation in humans.

body for years, working its way through until it strikes a vital organ and kills the dolphin. A poison gland associated with the spine exudes a venom that not only makes the sting extremely painful, but also causes the flesh to die around the wound, which often becomes septic as a result. A good treatment for a person who steps on a ray, or otherwise manages to get stung, is to soak the affected part in water as hot as the victim can stand. Most of the components of the venom are proteins broken down by heat.

Proteins can also be broken down by enzymes, including those that are conveniently bottled and sold as meat tenderizer. This is the preferred treatment for envenomation by sea jellies, hydroids, anemones, corals, and their relatives. Many of these animals use their harpoonlike stinging cells as offensive weapons to capture prey, but they become very useful as defensive weapons, too.

Poison-fang blennies have a single long fang with a venom gland at the back of each jaw. If a larger fish takes a poison-fang blenny into its mouth, the blenny bites it, and it spits the blenny out immediately. The predator seems to react only to the pain of the injury, since it responds before the venom would

The venomous spine at the base of a stingray's tail is strictly a defensive weapon. When molested, the stingray flexes its body and attempts to drive the spine into its attacker. If it punctures a vital organ, the spine can cause death.

have time to act. Which raises the question, what is the poison for? It may serve chiefly as a "forget-me-not" to make sure the predator learns to leave that type of blenny alone in the future.

POISON PISCES. Some fish do not have venomous weapons but are poisonous if eaten. Most trunkfish, lampreys, and hagfish exude a noxious mucus from their skin. They may do this only under stress. Aquarium owners are sometimes surprised when all of their fish suddenly die except for the trunkfish, which got stressed out and secreted its mucus into the tank. If the concentration of poison is high enough, it will kill the trunkfish, too. Boxfish have an additional defense in

198

the form of an external skeleton of interlocking bony plates, which gives them their unusual shape. Some of them, known as cowfish, also have a pair of hornlike projections on the head.

Many puffer fishes are poisonous, but this is not their only defense. When attacked, they swallow water and inflate themselves up to three times their normal size, making it impossible for the predator to swallow them. Some species have spines that lie flat against the body most of the time but are erected when

Above: *Slow-moving puffer fish are protected by the deadly poison tetrodotoxin, which is concentrated in the internal organs.* Opposite: *The first line of defense for a puffer fish is to inflate itself with water, making it impossible for a predator to swallow it.*

Death on a Dinner Plate

Some puffer fish are highly poisonous, but the toxins are concentrated in the internal organs. The puffer known as fugu in Japan is considered a great delicacy. If properly prepared, with all the internal organs carefully removed, just enough toxin is left in the flesh to give the diner a slight buzz. After eating fugu some aficionados report a floating sensation. Sometimes a little too much toxin is left, and the diner dies. To prepare fugu a chef needs a special license requiring more than a year of study. Nonetheless there are several fatalities each year. The final exam consists of preparing and consuming a meal of fugu.

Curiously, the poison in fugu is not produced by the fish itself but comes from bacteria growing on a type of algae the puffer fish eat. One story goes that some years ago, a gang of *yakuza* (Japanese gangsters) found out that this type of algae does not grow in one of the inland seas in Japan, and that therefore the fugu there are not poisonous. Supposedly they used this information to perpetrate the biggest mass murder in Japanese history. According to the story, a rival gang was invited to a dinner at which whole fugu were served. The hosts ate theirs with relish, knowing that the fish on their plates had come from the inland sea. The guests, in order to save face and appear just as fearless as their hosts, also finished their plates. Their fish, however, had come from the ocean.

the fish inflates, turning it into a spiky ball. This type of puffer is aptly named the porcupine fish.

The bacteria that puffer fish derive their poison from are also found in the internal organs of blue-ringed octopuses, horseshoe crabs, red coral crabs, and brown sea stars, rendering all of these animals poisonous to eat. The blue-ringed octopus also contains at least three other kinds of poison-producing bacteria. Poison is found in the octopus's tentacles, intestines, ink sac, salivary glands, and eggs. It can inject its poisonous saliva into a wound created with its sharp beak, both for self-defense and to immobilize prey. The presence of toxins in the ink sac suggests the intriguing possibility that the octopus may also be able to use "nerve gas." And by depositing poison in the eggs, it protects its offspring as well as itself.

WARNING SIGNALS. Some fish, and other animals, are brightly colored all the time, not just when they want to startle something. Fish use body colors and patterns for species recognition and social communication. They may be able to afford to risk a bright color pattern if they live close to the reef, where they can dash into a safe haven when danger threatens. For some creatures, though, a bright color pattern may be an important part of their defense. It sends a warning to the predator about some other defensive weapon they have. It doesn't do much good to be poisonous, for example, if a predator can't tell you apart from the other species on the reef and has to eat you to realize that it has made a mistake. A bright color may serve as a deterrent.

Caribbean reefs owe much of their color to the lovely sponges festooning the reef in hues of red, yellow, orange, and purple. On land, many of the beautiful colors we see are advertisements from flowers to pollinating insects, asking for some help with their reproduction. But underwater, most bright colors are warning signs. Many sponges are loaded with noxious chemicals and needlelike spicules, and they want predators to know about these before they take a bite out. Most sponges pose no threat unless they are eaten, but a couple of kinds can cause a severe irritation if a diver brushes against them. These are the fire sponge and the "touch-me-not" or "dread red" sponge. It is no accident that these are both red—the universal warning color. Both mothers and dive guides tell their charges, "If it's red, don't touch it." Since these two sponges grow in shallow water, the red color is visible even underwater.

Nudibranchs are essentially marine snails without shells. They actually have shells in their larval form, but they lose them as adults. They probably could not

Left: *A juvenile reef octopus hides among a cluster of multicolored sponges. Medical researchers are studying the defensive compounds produced by sponges to see if they have value in fighting cancer or other diseases.* Below: *Although sponges are abundant animals on most reefs and unable to hide or flee, they are exploited as a food resource by only a few animals, such as angelfish and hawksbill turtles. Most other predators are unable to deal with the toxic chemicals that the sponges produce.*

survive this loss if they didn't compensate with another defensive mechanism. Nudibranchs are favorites with divers because of the bright and distinctive color patterns many of them exhibit. Not too surprisingly, they usually contain lots of noxious defensive chemicals. A fish taking a nudibranch into its mouth usually spits it right back out again. The noxious substance may be throughout the nudibranch's body, or it might be secreted from glands on the animal's back. In one type of nudibranch, the glands are concentrated on a lump sticking up from the animal's back. Apparently this is used as a sacrificial lure. A predator will attack this area first, get a bad taste in its mouth, and give up on the rest of the animal.

Some nudibranchs exude a poisonous or foul-tasting mucus. The "stinky finger" nudibranch leaves a nasty smell on the finger of any person who touches it. A solution of two percent of its mucus in seawater will kill both fish and crustaceans. Another kind of nudibranch secretes sulfuric acid from skin glands when disturbed. Still others have daggerlike limestone spicules embedded in raised projections on the back. Some nudibranchs depend upon camouflage instead of warning colors. They merely absorb the color of the sponge or anemone that they are feeding on and become virtually invisible as long as they remain on it.

The gaudy blue polka dots of the blue-spotted fantail ray may well be a warning of its venomous tail spine. But why do all other stingrays wear drab

Opposite: *The bright colors of a nudibranch proclaim that it, too, is protected by noxious chemical compounds. Fish that attempt to prey on nudibranchs will usually spit them out.* Below: *Certain nudibranchs feed mostly on sponges. The sponges provide not only nutrition, but also noxious and toxic chemicals, which the nudibranch assimilates into its body and uses for its own defense.*

camouflage colors while this one wears what looks like a clown suit? As yet, scientists don't have a clue.

The most common kind of sea snake found on coral reefs advertises its venom with a black-and-white banded pattern. Most predators have such an aversion to this pattern that they will avoid any object painted with black-and-white bands. However, sea snakes do not occur in the Atlantic. In one experiment, researchers dropped sea snakes into separate tanks containing fish native

The blue-spotted fantail ray's bright blue spots may serve to warn predators of its venomous tail spine. But other stingrays, equally well armed, use camouflage for protection rather than warning colors.

The banded pattern of this venomous sea snake is a warning signal that fish within its range have learned to avoid. In areas where sea snakes do not occur, fish do not avoid objects with banded patterns.

to the Pacific and fish native to the Atlantic. The Pacific fish avoided the snakes, while the Atlantic fish attacked them and were often bitten and killed.

COPYCATS. You don't have to actually produce a poison as long as you can make your enemies think you have one. It's not surprising that some perfectly harmless animals have evolved a coloration very similar to that of more danger-ous ones to fool predators into leaving them alone. On land, the innocuous king snake has evolved a banded pattern very similar to that of the deadly coral snake. In the sea, the harmless banded snake eel is a perfect copy of the lethal banded

sea snake. The small black-banded sharp-nose puffer fish contains the same deadly poison as fugu. Its banded pattern is easily recognized by predators, who leave it alone. The little filefish called a mimic leatherjacket mimics this pattern so perfectly that even ichthyologists have been fooled. Although harmless, it enjoys the same protection from predation as the black-banded puffer.

The weever fish of the North Atlantic lies half-buried on the bottom. Under threat, it raises its dorsal fin, which is black, to point its venomous spines at the intruder. The common sole found in the same waters also buries itself partially in the bottom. If molested, it also raises a black fin. However, in this case, it is all bluff. Venomous scorpionfish are mimicked by basslets and cardinalfish. In an odd case of a mollusk pretending to be a fish, the banded octopus mimics the pattern of the venomous lionfish.

The wrasse blenny of the Caribbean mimics the color pattern and behavior of the juvenile bluehead wrasse, a cleaner. Predators do not harm it, because they need cleaners to keep them free of parasites. In this case, the blenny uses its mimicry only to avoid predation. The saber-toothed blenny of the Indo-Pacific takes it a bit farther. It mimics both the color and the swimming motion of the cleaner wrasse. When a larger fish approaches to have its parasites removed, the blenny dashes forward and takes a bite of skin before its victim realizes what is happening. Neither the saber-toothed nor the wrasse blenny depend totally upon their disguise, though.

Double-duty Deception

Several small blennies mimic the appearance of various species of poison-fang blennies. The poison-fang blennies use their venom for defensive purposes only and are not aggressive. Their fangs are not used in feeding. They feed only on small plankton and bottom-dwelling invertebrates. Larger fish need not fear them at all.

Some of their mimics, however, feed on skin, scales, and mucus, which they obtain by attacking larger fish. Their copycat color pattern gives the mimics two advantages: immunity from predation and a ruse to approach larger fishes. These fishes have no reason to avoid the true poison-fang blennies. The victims are taken by surprise when the mimics swim up and bite them. The aggressive mimics are much less common than the true poison-fang blennies; otherwise fish would learn to avoid them.

Mimic blenny

Opposite: *The banded toby carries the deadly poison tetrodotoxin in its skin and internal organs. The toby is mimicked by a small filefish that carries no poison, but it looks so similar to the toby that predators avoid it anyway.*

The saber-toothed blenny looks and swims just like a cleaner wrasse. When not at work, however, its identity is given away by its habit of using empty shells for burrows.

Both duck into a burrow when they feel threatened.

It can be protection enough just to resemble something uninteresting and inedible. The leaf fish looks exactly like a leaf and mimics one by swaying from side to side; sometimes it turns on its side and drifts back and forth in the surge. Juvenile Pacific batfish and Atlantic leatherjackets live along the fringes of mangrove swamps in their respective oceans. Both bear a remarkable resemblance to the fading leaves of the mangrove trees. They look nothing like the adults of their species, which are found farther from shore. If approached by a larger fish (or a diver), they often keel over and play dead, drifting like a leaf that has fallen into the water. The juvenile tripletail accomplishes the same trick even though it lives in the open ocean. It turns on its side while drifting with clumps of seaweed, which it closely resembles.

TRICK OR TREAT. Some color patterns do not disguise the fish as something else but merely break up its shape to make it hard to recognize as a fish. Bands (vertical lines) and stripes (horizontal lines) are the most common methods of

This leaf scorpionfish is almost invisible in its hiding place on the coral reef. Its scales have been modified through evolution into skin flaps that help to camouflage it.

achieving this sort of disguise, known as disruptive coloration. Stripes may be more effective for a fish swimming in the open, whereas bands may be a better disguise for a fish that is resting, especially if it is hiding among weeds or other cover. Fish able to change their color pattern may put on stripes when they are swimming and switch to bars when they stop moving.

An important part of a disruptive pattern is usually a mask that covers the eyes, most often a dark band. The eye is a key character that predators clue in on. It not only helps them identify their prey, but it also tells them if the prey can see

The false eyespots near the tails of these four-eye butterflyfish are believed to fool predators into striking at the wrong end of the fish. The illusion is aided by a dark band masking the real eye.

them and in which direction it will move. Some fish, such as the four-eye butter-
fly, complement their eye mask with a false eyespot that fools the predator into
thinking the tail end of the butterflyfish is actually the head. The predator attacks
toward the tail, perhaps attempting to lead the fish a little to intercept it as it
dashes to escape, and bites only empty water while the fish scoots off in the opposite direction.

Other fish, including the oval-spot butterflyfish and the juveniles of the
lemon peel and rock beauty angelfish, have a single very large dark spot roughly

*A predator attacking a swimming
fish has to lead the fish, aiming its
strike just ahead of the fish to intercept it. A false eyespot, such as the
one on this butterflyfish, can con-
vince a predator to strike behind the
fish, missing it entirely.*

in the center of each side of the body. This may appear like the eye of a much larger creature, making predators hesitant to attack.

At night, many predators, such as moray eels, hunt by smell, not by sight. This may be the reason that some parrotfish encase themselves in cocoons of mucus at night. The mucus sac may contain the odor of the parrotfish within it, preventing eels from finding the parrotfish. Another possibility is that the mucus cocoon prevents some of the smaller parasitic snails from reaching it. Both these ideas are purely speculation. The true function of the cocoon may still be a mystery. Not all parrotfish make these cocoons, and those that make them don't do so every night.

BAD COMPANY. Some animals without defenses gain protection not by mimicking better-armed creatures, but by associating with them. The man-of-war fish lives among the deadly tentacles of a Portuguese man-of-war. Various kinds of other small fish, usually juveniles, travel with other sea jellies, dashing into the tentacles or under the bell when danger threatens. These fish have acquired at least a partial immunity to the stings of their host, probably the same way anemonefish do to protect themselves from the stings of the anemones they live in (see Chapter 1, "Odd Couples"). A vari-

Opposite: *Nobody knows exactly why some parrotfish make mucus cocoons to sleep in at night. If the purpose is to prevent their scent from escaping, how can the bag contain their scent while letting in enough oxygen for respiration?*

A Portuguese man-of-war is accompanied by filefish and small man-of-war fish, which stay near the venomous tentacles of the man-of-war for protection from predators. The man-of-war fish are juvenile jacks, which will abandon the man-of-war when they grow larger.

ety of shrimps, fishes, and other small animals can be found hiding in anemones, corals, sponges, urchins, hydroids, and other animals that provide a defense against predation.

Golden zoanthids—tiny stinging relatives of corals—are often found growing on green rope sponges in the Caribbean. The zoanthids gain a surface to attach themselves to plus free food delivery, courtesy of the feeding currents created by the sponges. Both the zoanthids and the sponges feed on plankton drawn in by the sponge. The sponges benefit from the stinging defenses of the zoanthids and the defensive chemicals produced by the zoanthids. Even though sponges usually contain toxic chemicals of their own, they are preyed upon by angelfishes. Predation is greatly reduced, however, if the sponge is carrying zoanthids. The bright golden color of the zoanthid serves as a warning signal.

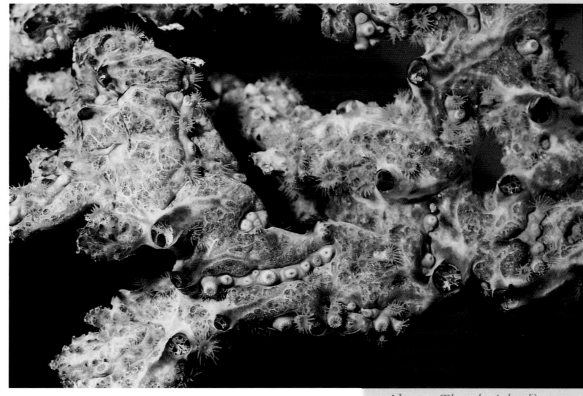

A similar relationship exists in the Pacific between certain corals and crabs and shrimp that live in them. The stinging cells of the coral are not adequate to protect it from the coral-eating crown-of-thorns starfish. But the crabs and shrimp can attack the starfish with their claws and drive it off. The crabs and shrimp are in no danger from the starfish, but they can be eaten by fish. The hard

Above: *The colonial golden zoanthids growing on this sponge produce toxic compounds, adding their stinging cells to the sponge's defensive arsenal. Sponges hosting zoanthids suffer considerably less predation from angelfish than those without.*
Left: *The crown-of-thorns sea star is a voracious predator of corals. It literally digests the living coral animals right out of their stony skeleton, which protects them from most predators.*

skeleton of the coral protects them from that danger. Together the coral and its crustacean tenants have an effective defensive alliance. Damselfish also protect corals that they live in, by biting attacking starfish, beating them with their tails, or physically picking them up and carrying them away. Some damselfishes also protect sponges in their territory from angelfish that try to feed on them.

KIDNAPPERS. Some animals are not content to just hang out with a protective host. They insist on taking their protection with them. It may provide camouflage, physical protection, chemical protection, defensive weapons, or a combina-

Guardian crabs living inside branching corals can actually protect them from attacks by crowns-of-thorns. When the sea star approaches the coral, the crab runs out and pinches the sea star until it changes direction.

tion of these. Decorator crabs have tiny hook-shaped bristles on their legs and back that work just like the fabric hook-and-loop fasteners found on clothing. They cover themselves with bits of algae, sponge, hydroids, and coral. This not only gives them the appearance of being just a little piece of reef, it also arms them with all the stinging cells and noxious chemicals of the hydroids, corals, and sponges they pick up.

Sponge crabs use only a piece of living sponge, which they trim to fit their shell. Carrier urchins pick up anything they can find on the bottom with the suction cups at the ends of their tube feet and stick it on their backs to hide themselves. They can be seen crawling around covered with bits of coral, sea grass, pebbles, leaves, and occasionally beer cans held tightly to their backs.

Hermit crabs borrow abandoned snail shells to use as mobile homes. These shells are much thicker and tougher than the crab's own shell, but they don't grow with the crab, so it has to keep moving into larger shells as it grows. Sometimes two hermit crabs will get into a ferocious battle over possession of a shell that each one fancies.

Since the hard shell may not be enough to deter all predators, some crabs take the extra step and plant some anemones on top to add a stinging deterrence.

The red-legged hermit crab has concealed its shell with an orange sponge, which adds the protection of the sponge's defensive chemicals. But the yellow nudibranch is eating the sponge, gaining the sponge's chemical defenses.

Stolen Weapons

Aeolid nudibranchs have rows of delicate-looking projections on their backs called cerata. Some of these nudibranchs feed on anemones, jellyfish, and hydroids, and somehow they prevent many of the stinging harpoons of these animals from firing when the nudibranch eats them. The stinging cells are not digested but pass through extensions of the gut up into the cerata. There they are redeployed in the defense of the nudibranch, and they will sting any other animal that attacks it. The purple pelagic

Pelagic nudibranch

nudibranch feeds on the tentacles of the Portuguese man-of-war as well as two other less potent sea jellies, but it retains only the more powerful man-of-war stingers for its defense. It can deliver a painful sting to a human.

How these slugs can eat and process the hair-trigger stinging cells without firing all of them is a complete mystery to biologists. It is also unknown how they avoid severe injury from the ones that do fire. Up to half of the stinging harpoons may be discharged during feeding and digestion. This defense is not always effective. The giant Atlantic nudibranch arms its cerata with the stinging cells of the anemones it feeds on. But New England lobsters have learned to just strip off the cerata and eat the rest of the body.

When they have to change shells, they carefully lift the anemones off the old shell and place them on the new one. The anemones apparently benefit from the free transportation and perhaps from scraps of the crab's meals. They release their grip when the crab taps them at the base and allow themselves to be moved without resistance. Boxer crabs place anemones right on their claws and wave them at anything that threatens.

GOING UNDERGROUND. Razor fish, a type of wrasse, have no weapons or elaborate disguises. And they live in open sand areas without shelter from predators. They have adapted to this high-risk situation by evolving an unusual head shape that permits them to dive right into the sand when threatened. They also live in colonies, which enhances their survival by allowing all the fish to be warned when any member of the colony detects a predator. They

reduce the need to go around looking for mates and exposing themselves to danger by breeding in harems. But the males are still at increased risk when they conduct their courtship displays. When predators are around, they perform these displays less often. But if the members of the harem do not receive enough attention, some of them

may change sex to become male. So predators threaten both the male razor fish's life and his breeding success.

Triggerfish dive not into the sand but into the coral when threatened. They wriggle their flattened bodies deep into a coral crevice, then erect a large spine on their dorsal fin, which makes them virtually impossible to extricate. The spine is locked up by an extension of a smaller spine behind it. The second spine gave the fish its name. Fishermen learned that it can be used like a trigger to release the larger spine that holds the fish in place.

Some fish, including stargazers, stingrays, and flounders, even though they may have defensive weapons or camouflage, often improve their odds by burying

Opposite: *Razorfish live over sandy bottoms. If threatened, they dive headfirst into the sand and disappear.* Above: *An eyed flounder matches its color and pattern almost perfectly to the sand bottom where it lies. If threatened, it will cover itself with sand to complete the disappearing act.*

in the sand with only their eyes exposed. Other fish, including jawfish, tilefish, and garden eels, dig burrows into the sand. Sometimes these burrows are quite elaborate, with multiple passages and entrances. Many wrasses bury in the sand at night to avoid predation while they are sleeping.

Above: *Stargazers have triple protection: camouflage, venom, and the ability to generate an electric shock. Some people might find the ugly face an adequate reason to leave these fish alone.* Opposite: *Christmas tree worms have no obvious eyes to enable them to see approaching predators, but pigment spots on the exposed radioles detect changes in light.*

DIGGING IN.

Invertebrates frequently create burrows as well. Ghost shrimps may dig the most extensive burrows relative to their size. Even though the shrimps are only an inch to a few inches long, their burrows can extend down ten feet or more, with many branches and at least two entrances. One entrance is usually level with the sand. The other has a raised mound built around it. This causes the current to accelerate as it passes over the entrance, creating a low pressure that pulls water through the burrow, ventilating it. This works on the same physical principle that allows boat sails and airplane wings to function.

Gall crabs do not dig burrows, but the females settle on the underside of a branching coral head. By irritating the coral, the crabs cause it to create a chamber, or gall, around them as it grows. Eventually the female crabs are trapped inside their chamber, though the dwarf males are able to move about freely. The trapped females are able to feed on tiny particles brought by the currents, and they can release their larvae into the same currents when they breed. But they can never leave their home as long as they live.

Christmas tree worms also create burrows in living coral heads, by secreting a smooth lining as the coral grows around them. They expose only their feathery gills for feeding and respiration. These are withdrawn very swiftly into the burrow when they sense water movement or a shadow passing over them.

Creatures that live in the open ocean cannot build burrows or dive into the sand to escape predation. But they can dive into the dark depths of the ocean. Many of the juvenile fish and small invertebrates that make up the plankton descend into deep water by day to avoid being spotted by visual predators and rise up to shallow water, where they can find more food, at night. Some of these creatures migrate thousands of feet twice a day. In some places

Some types of giant clams burrow into the coral, but the larger species lie exposed on the bottom. Their only defense is their heavy shells, which they snap shut at the approach of danger. Predation is high on small clams, but few animals can break the shell of a large one.

they are so thick that they reflect sonar signals, creating a "deep scattering layer." Their migrations confounded early oceanographers, whose depth-sounding equipment appeared to show an ocean that was inexplicably much shallower at night than it was during the day.

HARD BODIES.

Scallops have rows of very simple eyes, serving mainly to alert them to changing light levels that may signal the approach of a predator. When that happens, the two halves of the shell snap shut. Even giant clams weighing hundreds of pounds close their shells when they sense water movement. Nothing can get through the shell of a giant clam, which can be several inches thick, but their flesh is open to attack when the shell is open. Thorny oysters have long, bladelike spines that look as though they are designed to fend off predators. However, experiments have shown that the spines do not deter the animals that prey most often on the oysters. It seems that the real purpose of the spines is to attract the growth of sponges, which cover the oyster and conceal it.

Sea turtles, like clams and scallops, have shells made of two parts. But unlike land turtles, they are unable to pull their limbs and head completely inside

the shell. In addition, the shell on the underside is much softer than the one on top. If turtles cannot escape a predator, they turn the top of their shell toward it. A leatherback turtle was once filmed floating upside down at the surface to protect its soft underside from a tiger shark swimming beneath it.

The scales of most modern fish offer little protection against a larger animal with sharp teeth. But in ancient seas, most swimming animals were heavily armored. Some fish belonging to primitive families have retained the heavy-duty scales of their ancestors. These included tarpon, sturgeon, and garfishes. In the tropical Indo-Pacific, the giant bump-head parrotfish has evolved thick, hard scales that can deflect a steel spear fired from a powerful speargun at point-blank range. The scales are sometimes used by islanders as tools. Smaller individuals of the bump-head parrotfish hide inside the coral at night, like other parrotfish. But larger individuals are so sure of their invincibility that they often sleep right out in the open, lying upright on the sand.

Left: Giant clams protect their succulent mantle flesh with a heavy double shell, upon which corals, algae, and other organisms grow. The shell halves close together when the approach of a potential predator is detected. Below: Thorny oysters have spines on their shells that attract the growth of other organisms, which help to camouflage them. Rows of tiny eyes just inside the edge of the shell (next to the fringe of orange tentacles) detect changes in light and alert the oyster to close its shell.

Islanders sometimes capture them by reaching one arm under the fish's belly while it is asleep, putting the other hand on the forehead, and swimming them up to the boat or canoe.

Some barnacles have valves they can close to seal off the opening of their shell. If disturbed by a persistent predator, a barnacle can pull the valves in suddenly and squirt out a jet of water. If the barnacle has been exposed by a low tide, it can fire one of these water jets six feet through the air. If the predator is still undeterred, the barnacle may try to pinch it between the valves.

Above: By seizing the sculpin on the lip, this crab has temporarily avoided being swallowed. But if it lets go, it will become easy prey. Its next move will likely be to cast off its arm, leaving one claw to continue pinching the sculpin while the rest of the crab scuttles away. Right: A spotted yellowtail surgeonfish grazes on algae. This herbivore is not harmless, however. The three spines in front of the tail on each side can lacerate an attacker.

NUTCRACKERS AND SWITCHBLADES.
Crabs, lobsters, and some shrimp defend themselves very ably by pinching with their claws. In some species, the claws are not used for feeding but primarily for defense or for threat displays. Some crustaceans, such as the Maine

lobster and the mud crab or mangrove crab of the Indo-Pacific, have enormous claws that can break bones.

Surgeonfish are named for their defensive weapons—scalpel-sharp spines on the narrow part of the body just in front of the tail. Most surgeonfish have spines that work like switchblades. Most of the time they are folded down into a groove. When the fish is threatened, they can be erected and used to slash anything within reach. A few species have one or two pairs of large knifelike spines that are permanently erect. Some surgeonfish have bright colors on or around their spines to call attention to them.

One group of surgeonfish, the unicorn fish, have a large "horn" projecting from the front of the head, which must pose additional problems for any predator trying to swallow one.

The horn shark has a sharp, pointed spine just in front of its dorsal fin. The spine is erected when danger threatens, and it creates quite an unpleasant sensation for any creature trying to make a mouthful of one of these small sharks. Horn sharks are sometimes ambushed by angel sharks and sucked into the over-

A spotted unicorn fish sleeps in the coral at night. These fish receive their name from the horn on the forehead of most species. The purpose of this horn has not been fully explained, but it may serve as a defense against predators and make the fish more difficult to swallow.

Marching Lobsters

Spiny lobsters have no claws, but they have sharp spines on their shells and antennae. When threatened, they point their antennae at their attacker, which must risk impaling itself on the spines if it tries to approach closer. When spiny lobsters in the West Indies migrate across open bottom, they line up single file, with each lobster touching the one in front of it. This may provide some hydrodynamic advantage, but probably the main benefit is group defense. The file of lobsters, which can be hundreds of yards long, may appear as a single large animal to some predators. If the lobsters are attacked, they break formation and "circle the wagons," with their tails in the center and their

Spiny lobsters

antennae pointing out, presenting a forest of spines to the attacker. The "lobster march" is a movement of preadult lobsters from the shallow-water juvenile habitat to the deeper-water habitat they will use as adults. The march is triggered by the arrival of winter storms, which can create dangerous surge and waves in shallow water.

Opposite: This spotted porcelain crab may have cast off its other claw when attacked by a predator. Many crabs will pinch a predator before casting off a claw. The abandoned claw continues to pinch long after the crab has escaped, insuring that the predator's attention is distracted from the fleeing crab.

size mouths of these bottom-dwelling lurk-and-lunge feeders. Almost inevitably, the horn shark is spit back out a moment later, as soon as its horn contacts the roof of the angel shark's mouth.

DISPOSABLE LIMBS. Some animals, rather than fight to the death with a predator, prefer to give up part of themselves to save the rest. Crabs and lobsters may cast off a leg or claw when attacked. This is very different from having a claw broken off. If an appendage is broken off, it may leave an open wound that will cause bleeding and infection, and the crab will likely die. If the animal severs its own limb, it does it along a preset fracture plane, which is immediately sealed by a membrane. The missing part is regenerated over a period of time. In Florida stone crab fishermen take only the claws and throw the live animal back into the water to grow new ones. They must be very careful not to break the claws off themselves but merely induce the crab to release them. Sometimes crabs pinch an attacking organism and then release the claw. The separated claw continues to pinch the offender while the crab makes its escape.

Sea stars are also able to cast off arms and regenerate them. Brittle stars received their name because their arms come off so easily that they appear to be brittle. The cast-off arm continues to wriggle, to keep the predator's attention

A sea cucumber is covered with defensive filaments it has ejected as a defensive mechanism. These filaments, known as tubules of Cuvier, may be either sticky or poisonous.

while the brittle star crawls off to safety. Some species of sea stars can regenerate the whole animal from just the arm, in case the predator eats the wrong part.

Perhaps the most unlikely defense is the one used by some sea cucumbers. When threatened they may eject their internal organs toward the attacker, giving it something to munch on while the cucumber crawls off to regenerate new ones.

Other types of sea cucumbers eject sticky threads onto animals that molest them, an unpleasant experience that may lead the predator to avoid cucumbers in the future.

FLIGHT. Many animals run rather than fight. When approached by a sea star, a scallop that has been lying still on the bottom for most of its life may suddenly start clapping its shells together like castanets and jetting around backward through the water column. Some sea anemones, when threatened, can detach themselves from the bottom and actually somersault out of the way. Conch shells hop away from danger, perhaps partly to avoid leaving a continuous mucus trail that a predator could follow.

Some needlefish and halfbeaks, when frightened, lift most of their body out of the water and propel themselves with only the lower part of the tail. The resistance of air is less than that of water, so they are able to attain a greater speed in their flight this way. Flying fish have evolved winglike pectoral fins that enable them to leave the water entirely and glide for up to a thousand feet. While it may appear that they are flying, they are actually only gliding. Their tails must propel them out of the water to begin the glide.

229

Flying fish glide on outstretched pectoral fins after leaping from the water. Since the lower lobe of the tail is longer than the upper, it can dip back into the water and propel the fish into the air again.

Secret Senses

If asked to choose one word to describe the sea, most people would pick "blue." Like the sky, the ocean at times seems to consist of a pervasive, all-encompassing blueness that almost drowns the senses in its intensity. Sometimes, looking at the surface of the sea from shore or from a boat, its color appears to be merely a re-flection of the color of the sky. When fluffy white clouds fill the sky on a wind-less day, the sea may look almost white if

The brilliant colors of the deep reef are visible only upon the addition of artificial light. Behind the orange sea fan, some branches shielded from the photographer's light show the "natural" color.

The dazzling colors of coral reef fish may serve social functions and as species recognition. But what of the equally vivid colors of corals and other nonsocial invertebrates? In some cases they warn predators of chemical defenses. In many cases they are unexplained.

its surface is smooth enough. On a completely overcast day, the ocean appears gray. But jump into the open ocean and look below the surface, even on the grayest, dreariest day, and the water regains the same intense blueness that it has on a cloudless day.

The ocean is blue because seawater absorbs different colors of light selectively. The colors of the spectrum are absorbed in the same order in which they appear in a rainbow. Red is absorbed most quickly, followed by orange, yellow,

green, blue, indigo, and finally violet. The more water that light of any color has to pass through, the more of it is absorbed. As sunlight passes into the ocean, most red light is absorbed by a depth of 30 feet. Deeper than 100 feet, most colors other than blue and violet have disappeared. The sensitivity of our own eyes does not extend far into the violet range, so we see mostly blue. This leads to some interesting visual anomalies. At a depth of 60 feet, a red sponge looks brown, but blood appears green. On the surface, the green pigments in blood are masked by the stronger red ones. When the red light is gone, the green color becomes visible.

DROWNED COLORS.

Scientists for many years assumed that fish and other marine creatures could see no colors and were sensitive only to blue light. Since blue is the primary color in the marine habitat, they reasoned that these animals would gain nothing by having color vision. Some fishes, such as tuna and marlin, which spend their entire lives in the open ocean, do see mostly in the blue part of the spectrum. But other fishes spend a lot of time in shallow water, where colors are visible. And what of the brilliant color patterns of tropical reef fish? What purpose could these serve if they could not be seen? And why should a frogfish

The psychedelic mandarin fish spends most of its time hidden within the coral rubble. It usually emerges to court a mate only in late afternoon or evening when its dazzling colors are almost invisible, making the evolution of such a bizarre design seem that much more improbable.

A Question of Color

Most invertebrates have much simpler eyes than those of fish and other animals with backbones. But octopus, squid, and cuttlefish have complex eyes very similar to those of vertebrates. These animals belong to a group of mollusks known as cephalopods. Since mollusks are believed to have evolved on a completely different path from vertebrates, the similarities are thought to be a case of separate groups independently arriving at the same solution to a biological challenge.

Cephalopod eyes are large and complex. At ten inches in diameter, the giant squid's eye is the largest in the animal kingdom. Cephalopods can discriminate very fine details, can adjust their pupils to control incoming light, and can focus from about one inch to infinity. But can they see color?

Cuttlefish

Examination of the structure of their eyes and visual pigments has led experts to conclude that most cephalopods almost certainly cannot. This creates a real problem in explaining some of their behavior. For example, some cephalopods can change color almost instantly to blend in with the background around them. How can they do this without being able to see the color of the background? It may be that they are primarily matching shades of light and dark. They also use reflecting cells, which automatically pick up the colors around them. However, it is very curious that color-blind animals should be covered with special color cells that enable them to produce yellow, green, red, pink, orange, brown, black, and white skin tones at will.

waste its energy matching its color to the sponge it is hiding on, if all its predators were color-blind?

Recent studies have shown that many fish do see colors quite well. In one experiment, bait fish were dyed red and treated with foul-tasting chemicals before being fed to gray snappers. The snappers refused red fish for a long time afterward. In other experiments fish learned to associate colored discs with food rewards. Sharks showed a preference for yellow in one study. Some kinds of dolphins have also shown the ability to discriminate between different colors.

In other animals, evidence for color vision comes from examination of the retinas and visual pigments of the eyes. Two types of light receptors occur in the retina—rods and cones. Rods are sensitive to very low levels of light and furnish greater detail, but they provide only black-and-white vision. Cones contribute color vision, but they require bright light to function. Animals that have only rods are assumed to see in black and white. Animals that have both rods and cones, and more than one visual pigment, are usually assumed to have color vision. Interestingly, the retina of one type of sea snake was found to contain only cones and no rods.

INVISIBLE LIGHT.

Not all seawater is blue. In coastal waters, suspended particles of organic matter may absorb blue light more strongly and cause green to become the dominant color. In swamps and other areas with a very high amount of silt and detritus, the water may appear brown, yellowish, reddish, or even black. The visual pigments in the eyes of fish living in these habitats correspond very well with the colors of light that are predominant.

Some fish are able to see parts of the color spectrum that are not visible to us. In shallow, swampy areas where silt and decaying vegetable matter make the water appear black, a human might not be able to see a hand in front of the face. Around dawn and dusk, when many of the fish are feeding, there might appear to be no light at all. But fish whose eyes are sensitive to infrared light are able to see.

Until recently ultraviolet light was believed to be absorbed very rapidly in seawater. Now we know that it penetrates more than 100 feet — deeper than most other colors. Ultraviolet light, which has a very short wavelength, is scattered less than visible light, and therefore penetrates better through murky water. But ultraviolet is invisible to the human eye. Because magnetic videotape is more sensitive to ultraviolet, underwater objects can sometimes be recorded on videotape even when they cannot be seen clearly. Some fish are also able to see ultraviolet light. Some fish can even locate and strike at prey when ultraviolet light is the only color of light present.

The discovery that ultraviolet light is transmitted through seawater explained the mystery of the colors that "weren't supposed to be there." Divers

Adjacent colonies of lettuce coral, shades of brown by daylight (top), *fluoresce blue and green under ultraviolet light* (bottom). *Colonies of the same species of coral may fluoresce different colors, or some colonies may fluoresce while others do not.*

were baffled to see bright red corals at depths of more than 100 feet. Theoretically, all of the red rays from the sunlight should have been absorbed at that depth. And sure enough, a red wet suit would appear dark maroon in the blue light filtering down from the surface. But the coral was unmistakably red. Even more curious, in flash photographs the red coral appeared green. This is also true of some anemones and other organisms that exhibit incongruously bright colors.

It turned out that the mystery colors are caused by fluorescence. Certain minerals and chemicals absorb energy from blue and ultraviolet light and reemit that energy in a different color. Fluorescence is what gives certain paints their bright, vibrant colors. By diving at night with black (ultraviolet) lights in watertight casings, divers discovered that a great many marine organisms, of all differ-

A cream-colored anemone (left) fluoresces blue-green when exposed to ultraviolet light (right). Many marine creatures exhibit fluorescence, but so do many minerals. Fluorescence may be just a result of the chemical composition of the animals and may confer no selective advantage.

ent types, fluoresce a variety of vibrant colors when exposed to ultraviolet light.

IN THE DEPTHS. Even blue, violet, and ultraviolet light do not reach far beyond the surface layers of the ocean. A human eye looking upward can detect a faint glow from the surface until reaching a depth of almost 2,000 feet. A few organisms with more sensitive eyes can perhaps detect light a little deeper. Some deepwater fish have tubular eyes, both of which are directed upward like periscopes toward the light coming down from the surface. The light at 2,275 feet is only one-tenth of one-billionth of the amount of light at the surface. Below 3,000 feet, sunlight does not penetrate. Yet the largest part of the ocean lies below that depth, with the deepest trench in excess of 35,000 feet. In this abyssal world of perpetual darkness, one might expect all the inhabitants to be blind, as they typically are in caves. But this is not the case.

Some deep-sea dwellers have atrophied eyes and depend on other senses. But some have normal-looking or even greatly enlarged eyes that are very sensitive to light. Some have color vision. In fact the only type of squid apparently able to see in color lives in the lightless ocean depths. Nature decrees that organs not used will be lost. These eyes must be seeing something, but it is not light coming from the sun. It is light produced in the depths by living creatures.

Many creatures of the depths—and creatures of the night—can produce chemical light similar to that made by a firefly or a chemical light stick. And they

At the end of the "fishing pole" sprouting from the forehead of this deep-sea anglerfish is a lure that glows in the dark to attract prey.

A deep-sea anglerfish attracts its prey with a bioluminescent lure that it wriggles from a long appendage on its forehead.

produce it the same way—by mixing two chemicals together. Those that cannot manufacture the chemicals themselves cultivate glowing bacteria to produce light. This phenomenon is called bioluminescence, which is not the same thing as fluorescence. Organisms use this chemical light to see, to communicate, to feed, and to confuse predators.

Most of the chemical light in the ocean is firefly green. And therefore most of the animals in the deep sea can see only in the blue-green part of the spectrum. But some can produce—and see—light in other colors, especially red. These animals have a "private communications channel" that their enemies cannot intercept. Some use their red lights like searchlights to hunt color-blind animals that do not even realize a light is shining on them. Some midwater fishes have yellow filters over their eyes that apparently help them see yellow and red luminescence better against the blue background.

AN EYE FOR EVERY OCCASION.

The visual capabilities of different organisms vary greatly. Some creatures, especially those living in caves and other environments where vision is of little use, are completely blind. Others have well-developed eyes that are extremely sensitive to light and form detailed images.

Some invertebrates have very simple eyes consisting only of pigment spots. They have no lens to focus an image and no pupil to regulate the amount of light reaching the pigment. These eyespots serve only to alert the organism of changes in light levels. Christmas tree worms, for example, have eyespots on their feathery gills, which alert the worm to approaching organisms by detecting the shadow. The worm responds by quickly withdrawing into its burrow. Many marine worms have two, four, six, or eight eyes.

Light from the Bottom of the Sea

In the middle of the Atlantic Ocean, 10,000 feet below the surface, hot, sulfurous brine spews out of cracks known as hydrothermal vents. Like oases in the abyss, these vents support a profusion of life. One inhabitant is a shrimp with light-sensitive spots on the back of its shell. Since these "eyes" have no lenses, they can't focus an image, but they must be there to detect light of some sort. Curious as to what the shrimp might be "seeing," scientists sent down instruments and discovered that red and infrared light is coming from the vents. There may even be enough to support photosynthesis, which so far is not known to occur without sunlight. What's making the light? Thermal radiation was ruled out. Too much light is produced for that explanation. It could be coming from energy released by collapsing gas bubbles, crystallizing or cracking minerals, or chemical reactions in the brine, but no one knows.

A feather duster worm's eyes respond only to changing light levels and do not allow the animal to perceive images. They are nonetheless critical for its survival, alerting the worm of the approach of a predator in time to pull its feathery plume back into the safety of the tube.

Some planktonic animals have only a single eye that measures light intensity. This enables the creature to migrate up and down with the change from day to night. Such animals often maintain themselves at a constant light level. They can be found deeper in the ocean on a night when the moon is full than when it is new and more shallow on a cloudy day than a sunny one. Some have eyes that respond to different colors of light and may function as a sort of depth gauge.

Some planktonic animals, however, have two or more eyes and may be able to discriminate the size and shape of objects, or even use their eyes in feeding.

Moon jellyfish have a ring of very simple eyes going around the edge of the bell. These probably serve only to measure light levels and help the jelly to maintain its orientation with respect to the surface, perhaps also to judge its depth. Box jellyfish have more complex eyes with a lens and retina, which are capable of focusing an image. The Australian box jelly, or sea wasp, responds to the light of a match at a distance of five feet.

Corals and anemones have no eyes or other sense organs. Yet they follow regular day-night cycles in feeding, and they synchronize their reproductive activity very precisely with both solar and lunar calendars. Many kinds of corals and anemones respond to lights shone on them at night, usually by closing up. Some respond to red light in the same way as to white light, proving that they can at least detect this color, but not necessarily distinguish it from other colors.

The eyes of some marine snails are little more than pits lined with visual pigments. Others have telescopic eyes comparable to those of many fishes. Scallops have perhaps the most striking eyes in the animal kingdom—two rows of up

Opposite: *Moon jellyfish have very simple eyes. They are not able to form images but merely determine light intensity and direction.* Above: *The scallop's eyes are interspersed with sensory tentacles, which detect water motion and aid the eyes in determining when to clamp the shells shut. The violet cap on top of this scallop is an encrusting sponge.*

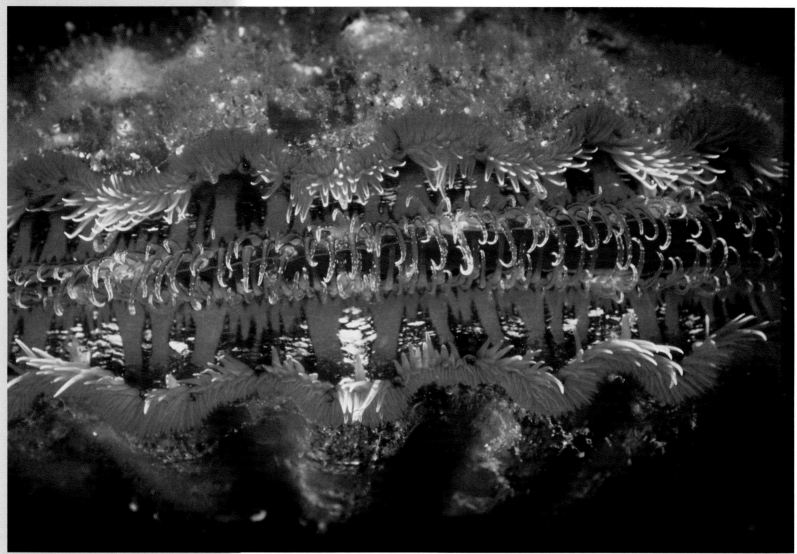

Scallops have up to 50 spherical eyes along the lips of their shells. These "beautiful blues" do not enable it to see its surroundings but rather function something like an electric eye that opens and shuts an automatic door.

to 50 bright red or blue eyes each, looking out of the opening between the two shells. These beautiful spherical eyes serve only to respond to sudden changes in light levels and alert the scallop when to snap its shell shut to stay out of trouble.

MORE COMPLEX EYES. Most crustaceans, such as crabs, shrimp, and lobsters, have compound eyes similar to those of insects. These are composed of cylindrical units, each with its own lens and light receptor. Maine lobsters have as many as 14,000 of these units in each eye. The images from each unit are probably combined into a sort of mosaic. The eyes are often carried on stalks, giving the animal an extremely wide view, sometimes surpassing 180 degrees. However, they apparently do not resolve very detailed images and cannot see very far away.

The design of the lobster eye is being used to build a new X-ray telescope, which will be able to view a much larger area of the sky than previous designs. The Lobster Eye telescope will be carried on a small satellite and is expected to be able to accomplish in weeks surveys that previously took years.

Mantis shrimps have complex eyes composed of thousands of units each. The eyes are the primary organs used in coordinating prey capture. Mantis shrimps are both highly accurate and extremely fast in their strikes. A strike can be executed in less than $\frac{1}{200}$ of a second, and the shrimp almost never misses. They are able to judge the position and size of prey very

Above: *The molted shell of a spiny lobster includes clear, hard coverings for the stalked eyes. The compound structure of the eyes can be seen even in the discarded shell.* Left: *The bean-shaped compound eyes of the giant mantis shrimp, enormous relative to its body size, are divided in the middle by a band of specialized cells. If two halves of the eye can form separate images, this could explain how mantis shrimps can judge distance accurately with only one eye.*

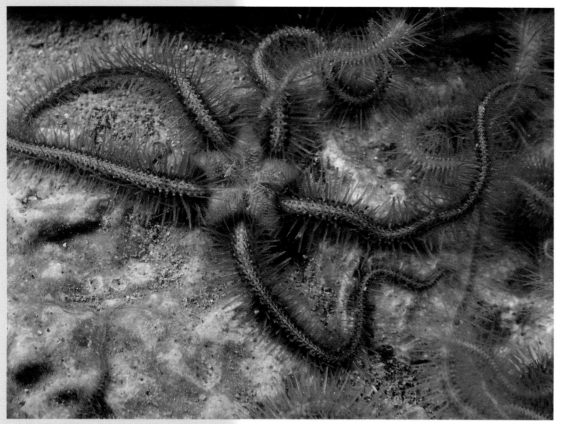

precisely, even if they have only one eye, and they do not confuse size and distance. How they can do this without requiring input from both eyes has not been explained.

The eyestalks of crustaceans are complex organs. They may have many duties other than vision, including production of reproductive hormones. This is not as surprising as it might seem, since many animals time their reproductive cycles according to day length, lunar phase, or other changes in light cycles. Aquaculturists sometimes induce shrimp to spawn by removing one or both eyestalks.

Above: *Though brittle stars have no eyes, they are negatively phototactic—that is, they move away from a source of light, usually crawling under the nearest rock or piece of coral.* Right: *No eyes or other sense organs have been found in basket stars. Yet they react very strongly to light. At night the basket star untangles its branched arms and spreads them out fanlike to catch plankton. The brief flash of a dive light causes the arms to curl up again.*

Some sea stars have simple eyes at the tips of their arms. It is supposed that they use these only to respond to changing levels of light—hiding themselves or coming out to feed at the appropriate time of day or night. However, they respond to light in the same way even when the eyes are covered. The entire surface of the skin is believed to act as a photoreceptor organ. This may be the case

for brittle stars and basket stars, because they respond very strongly to light—crawling quickly under the nearest shelter whenever light is present.

The photoreceptors of sea urchins are believed to be individual nerve cells. Most urchins and some sea cucumbers respond to light like brittle stars, by hiding themselves. Yet only a few sea cucumbers have anything that can be identified as a visual organ. Those that do have eyespots belong to the group of sea cucumbers that are most responsive to light. Some of these withdraw into a hiding place in seconds when struck by a light beam.

FISH-EYE VIEW.

Though the eyes of fish are quite similar to our own, there are important differences. Fish cannot adjust focus by changing the shape of the eye lens the way we do. Instead the lens is pulled back and forth. And most fish, apart from sharks, cannot change the size of their pupil to control the amount of light coming in. Nor do most fish have eyelids.

Sharks are fishes, but unlike most other fishes, they can contract their pupils to adjust to light differences between day and night. This enables them to hunt at any time of day, unlike most fishes, which are active either by day or by

The eyes of balloonfish and some other puffers often have blue-green iridescent specks in the pupil. How these affect the fish's vision, or what purpose they may serve, is unknown.

A finely tuned array of sensory capabilities enables sharks to stay on top of the food chain as apex predators. The struggle for survival constantly pits the sensory abilities of the predator against those of the prey.

night. Many sharks also have a membrane that functions like an eyelid to protect the eye, except that it closes from the bottom rather than the top.

A reflective layer at the back of sharks' eyes effectively doubles the amount of light striking the photoreceptors. At night, light reflects back out of the eyes of sharks just as it does with cats and other nocturnal creatures. Experts believe sharks can hunt by starlight on a moonless night. Measurements indicate that some sharks are farsighted. Their vision is acute for objects at a distance, but it may be a little fuzzy for things that are close up. At close range sharks tend to depend more upon other senses. They often close their eyes to prevent injury when they attack prey, depending entirely upon their other senses to orient them.

Like their relatives the sharks, rays are fishes, but unlike sharks they cannot change the size of their pupils. Instead, they have a structure working something like a fringed curtain that lowers over the pupil in bright light. The "fringes" shield the eye from excessive light, but they also effectively split the pupil into several smaller openings. This may increase the depth of field of the ray's vision. In eyes, as in cameras, the smaller the hole through which the light enters, the greater the range of distance in focus.

Rays cannot change the size of their pupils. Instead they have a flap that covers and uncovers the pupil to control the amount of light entering.

Most fish have one eye on each side of the body, and the range of vision of the two eyes overlaps just a little in the front.

Perhaps the most important difference between fish eyes and our own is the fish's ability to use its eyes independently. Our eyes are linked together to give us binocular vision, which allows us to judge distance. This, however, gives us a limited field of view. We see only what is in front of us. In the ocean it is extremely important to see what is coming at you from all sides. Not having necks, fish are unable to turn their heads. Some bottom-dwelling and deep-sea fish have eyes on the tops of their heads, but most fish have their eyes on the side.

Most fishes' eyes bulge out, giving them a "fish-eye view" of 160 to 180 degrees on each side. Most fishes have a small amount of overlap in front, giving them binocular vision over a small angle ahead of them. Otherwise each eye takes in a separate view, meaning that a fish may be seeing nearly 360 degrees around itself at once. The small blind spot in back is compensated by sinuous swimming or alternating head and eye movements. Most fishes with movable eyes can rotate them independently. It can be quite disconcerting to watch a small blenny move its eyes around in all different directions at once.

KEEPING AN EYE OUT. In some fish, the two eyes have different functions. In one of the deepwater fishes, one eye is directed upward to gauge the dim light coming down from the surface, while the other is directed forward to watch for light generated by other organisms. Only one eye of a flounder senses the color pattern of the substrate the flounder is resting on. If that eye is covered, the flounder is unable to match its own color to the background. In the four-eyed

A peacock flounder's eyes are raised on stalks to give it a better view of its surroundings and allow the flounder to bury itself in the sand, leaving its eyes exposed. Like those of many fish, the flounder's eyes can see and rotate independently, giving it a 360-degree panorama.

fish, found in Trinidad, both eyes are split into two parts, including the lens and retina. One part sees above water, as the fish swims, and the other sees underwater. The two parts of the lens are of different thicknesses, so the fish can see sharply in air and water at the same time.

Since the two eyes of a fish have different views, their vision is two-dimensional on each side. They cannot judge the distance of an object to the side by comparing the views from two eyes. Swimming fish, however, can judge the distance of an object by its relative apparent motion. Just as trees close to the road apparently whiz by a moving vehicle much faster than trees farther away, things close to a swimming fish move more quickly across its visual field than more distant objects. Relative size—closer objects appear larger—is useful only if the fish already knows the size of the object it is looking at.

The eyes are not the only light-receptive organs in fish. Larval lampreys have light-sensitive spots on their tails. When light is detected, they burrow deeper into the bottom sediments. Larval herring migrate up and down in response to changing light levels. But they do this even when their eyes have been removed. How they sense the light is not certain. Some types of fish have translucent skulls that allow light to penetrate to the pineal and parietal organs, outgrowths of the forebrain. They have no structures, such as a lens, that would allow these organs to create an image, and their exact function is unknown. Probably they serve to measure

Fish with Sunglasses

Most light consists of waves moving in many different planes all traveling together at the same time. Sometimes light is reflected in such a way that all the light waves are lined up so that they are propagating in the same plane of travel. We call this light polarized. Our eyes cannot detect polarization without the aid of polarized sunglasses or similar filters. Some animals, however, have this ability. Honeybees and other insects use patterns of polarized light in the sky for navigation.

Recently some fish were shown to have this capability as well. Fish living in shallow water can see the sky through the surface of the water. Changing patterns of polarization as the sun moves through the sky apparently enable these fish to tell direction and follow daily migration patterns. Light entering the water also becomes polarized in the direction of the sun. This may help fish that cannot see the sky determine the direction of the sun and use it as a compass. Salmon, halfbeaks, and leaf fish have been shown to orient to polarized light. Cephalopods can also see polarized light. This probably enables them to see fish better, since light is polarized when it reflects off fish scales.

Amazon river dolphins are rarely found in water this clear. In the normally murky water of the Amazon and Orinoco rivers and their tributaries, vision is of limited use. These dolphins can see, but they have very small eyes and depend more on their senses of hearing and touch.

day length, lunar cycles, ambient light levels, or other environmental data. They may use this information to regulate hormone levels in the brain related to daily activity patterns, reproductive cycles, or other functions.

Seabirds that dive for fish require excellent vision above water to locate their prey, but they must also have perfect vision underwater in order to seize it. In some birds that have been studied, this is accomplished by a flattening of the eye when they dive.

Most marine mammals have good to excellent vision, and at least some are known to discriminate colors. The eyes of river dolphins, though, have degener-

Above: *Orcas and other marine mammals sometimes "spyhop" to look around above the water.* Opposite: *Sea lions are able to see in front of themselves with both eyes at the same time. This binocular vision enables them to judge distance.*

ated to the point that the dolphins are probably functionally blind. Vision is of little use in the murky rivers where these animals live, so they must rely on other senses. Most dolphins and whales, however, have excellent vision, both in water and in air. The lens of the eye is highly elastic, allowing it to change shape enough to focus accurately when the animal sticks its head out of the water. Some species do this occasionally and have a look around above the surface. This is called spyhopping.

Oddly enough, seals, which spend more time above water, are astigmatic in air and see well only underwater. Seals, otters, and sea lions have the eyes toward the front of the head for good binocular vision. Whales and dolphins have the eyes placed on the sides of the head, like fish. Some whales have a blind spot directly ahead of them. This does not prevent them from knowing what is in front of them, though, for this is precisely the direction in which other sensory systems are most effective.

GOOD VIBRATIONS.

For humans, sight is the most important and most developed of all the senses. Sight can give us critical information about things happening a great distance away. In the ocean this is not possible. Light is rapidly weakened, and vision is restricted to short distances. Sound waves, on the other hand, travel five times faster and carry much farther in water than in air. And they can deliver information across much greater distances in water than can light waves.

Naturally, marine creatures have adapted their sensory systems to the characteristics of their environment. And each organism depends most upon

The group of fish known as grunts receive their common name from the distress calls they make when captured. The extent to which they use sound to communicate underwater is uncertain. The center fish, which appears to be speaking, is actually "yawning."

those senses most important to its particular lifestyle and habitat. Different land animals rely more heavily on different senses—bears depend on smell; bats rely on hearing. In the same way, different marine animals make more or less use of the various senses depending on their particular needs. They also use senses that we don't even have.

The lines between some of the senses are somewhat blurred underwater. Because water is viscous, it becomes difficult to distinguish between taste and smell and between touch and hearing. The difference between a sound wave and a pressure wave is academic. Fishes use both their ears and sensors on the rest of

their bodies to detect vibrations in the water. Instead of an eardrum, fish have a spherical ear bone to transfer sound vibrations to the nerve cells that carry sound signals to the brain. Since a fish's body is mostly water and is not rooted to anything, it moves back and forth with the sound waves passing through it. The ear bone is about three times the density of the fish's body. Inertia tends to hold it still while the fish's body vibrates back and forth around it. The movement of the ear bone relative to the body bends surrounding bristles attached to nerve endings, which carry the sound to the brain. In some fishes, the air bladder, which provides buoyancy, also acts as a resonator to help translate sounds to the ear.

DETECTION METHODS.

Other nerves end in sensory hairs scattered about the heads of most fish and concentrated in a canal running down the length of the fish's body on each side. This is called the lateral line. This special sense organ, found only in fish, is most useful for detecting vibrations from the swimming motions of other fish and from similar disturbances. It is believed to be critical for the orientation

Fishes detect vibrations in the water, not only with their inner ears, but also with other sensors.

and spacing of fish in schools, although sight is important as well. The lateral line may explain how all the fish in a school seem to turn simultaneously. It provides

what has been called a "distant touch" sense for detecting low-frequency sounds and pressure waves. These cells are not sensitive to temperature changes, which are detected by other nerve endings in the skin, as are physical touches. So touch can still be distinguished as a separate sense.

Right: The lateral line of this "big eye" is visible as a curved stripe, slightly lighter in color than the rest of the fish, arching down from just behind the gill plate and running back to the tail. Below: *These margates (a type of grunt) use their lateral lines to sense the position of the other fish in the school.*

Most fish probably use the lateral line system to help them avoid predators. Some use it as well to help them find prey: Sharks are strongly attracted to speakers broadcasting irregularly pulsed low-frequency sounds. The same sort of sounds are created by the erratic swimming of an injured fish.

Since nearly every aquatic animal has to be concerned about swimming predators, most have some method of detecting water motion. The motion detectors

Cuttlefish have color cells in their skin that enable them to produce a wide variety of colors, changing their color, pattern, and even texture almost instantaneously. But studies indicate that they themselves cannot see colors.

on a crayfish are special cells on the tail fan that end in fine hairs less than one tenth of a millimeter long. These respond to a movement as slight as one-millionth of a millimeter. Squid and cuttlefish have rows of hair cells on their heads and arms so sensitive to water movement that they can detect a fish swimming 100 feet away.

SOUND SYSTEMS. The use of sound underwater is developed to its highest degree in marine mammals, particularly in cetaceans—whales, dolphins, and porpoises. Their range of hearing and sound production extends well above and below what we can hear. Common dolphins can hear sounds at frequencies three times lower and ten times higher than humans' hearing range. They can detect sounds one and a half octaves above the highest sound that a dog can register.

Cetaceans can also locate the direction sounds are coming from underwater, which we cannot. Our skulls reflect sounds arriving in air, so that sound waves come in only at our ears. But underwater our skulls transmit sound waves to us, so that they arrive at both ears almost simultaneously. The ears of cetaceans, however, are insulated from the skull by foam-filled air spaces. Their ears are almost invisible from the outside—just pinholes behind the eyes. Evidence is mounting that sounds are picked up and transferred to the ears by the lower jaw.

ANIMAL SONAR.

Dolphins and toothed whales use sound to learn about their world not just by passive listening but by active interrogation. They send out series of clicks that reflect off objects and return to them, allowing them to derive detailed information about the object. This process, called echolocation, works the same way as sonar on a submarine. Apparently dolphins can formulate much more detailed images with their echolocation than are possible with any sonar that has been devised by man. Since sound can penetrate tissues, dolphins can likely "see" inside each other's bodies in the same way that ultrasound scans are used in hospitals. It has been speculated that dolphins use echolocation to exam-

A spotted dolphin examines the photographer visually during a close pass. Before approaching this close, the dolphin may have "scanned" the photographer at a distance with its echolocation clicks.

ine each other's internal organs and determine the state of another dolphin's health, emotions, reproductive condition, and so forth. A pregnancy could be detected almost immediately.

Scientists believe that the echolocation sounds are made by moving air back and forth between internal spaces in the head and that they are focused through the fatty area on the forehead called the melon. But the exact details of how the sounds are produced remain a mystery. The sound is somehow focused into a narrow beam that the dolphin can direct with its head and use to locate prey as well as to avoid predators. Fish have air bladders, which reflect sound, making them highly visible targets for echolocation.

Squid, however, do not have air bladders. Their bodies are almost exactly the same density as water, so in theory sound waves should pass right through them, leaving them "invisible" to echolocation. Yet some dolphins feed on squid in the dark of night. Pilot whales feed mostly on squid, and sperm whales feed almost exclusively on squid, diving to depths of one or two miles for them—much deeper than sunlight penetrates. Furthermore, their eyes are positioned so that they probably can't see directly in front of their jaw. While they are diving, they make regular loud clangs, which are generally believed to be echolocation noises. But if squid do not reflect sound, how do the noises help? If sperm

Flipper Goes for the Gold

The echolocation signals of dolphins can penetrate a short distance into sand on the ocean floor. Some groups of spotted and bottlenose dolphins feed regularly on small fish that bury in the bottom. These fish are invisible to most predators, but not to the dolphins, which position themselves head down and scan the bottom with their signals until they locate a fish. In order to retrieve the fish, the dolphins sometimes dig down until their heads are completely buried, leaving craters in the seafloor where they have fed.

Reflected sound signals can give a dolphin information not only about the position and shape of an object but also its composition. Dolphins can easily be trained to identify different types of metals. Many anecdotal stories tell of both captive and wild dolphins

Bottlenose dolphin digging out a fish

finding and returning valuable lost objects such as watches, tools, and jewelry. These stories were not lost on treasure hunters frustrated with the inability of their own expensive electronic search equipment to differentiate between gold or silver and worthless metals such as iron. Needless to say, they attempted to enlist trained dolphins as scouts in treasure-salvage operations. Unfortunately for the treasure hunters, the dolphins' "sonar" cannot penetrate the bottom sediments to more than a foot or so. Most sunken treasure is buried deeper than that.

whales do not find squid by echolocation, how do they locate them? Some scientists have proposed that the sperm whales are not finding the squid at all but rather somehow attracting the squid into their mouths. For the present, the question of how the sperm whale finds its dinner in the inky darkness of the abyss remains a mystery.

Scientists are equally divided about the question of whether or not dolphins and whales can use sound to stun or kill their prey as well as to locate it. Certainly they are capable of making very loud noises. Once when a sperm whale stranded itself on a beach, one of the rescuers reported that every time it made a "clang," her hand was pushed off its forehead.

SEEING WITH SOUND. Baleen whales are not toothed whales; they have comblike filters rather than teeth for feeding. They also make many noises, some of them very loud, but they do not make the sequences of clicks used by toothed whales and dolphins for echolocation. Yet they exhibit such impressive navigational and prey-finding abilities that some people still insist they must have some form of sonar.

Dolphins also have shown evidence of being able to track fish without sending

Opposite: *This juvenile sperm whale has a number of "hitchhiking" remoras clinging to it. When it is old enough to dive deep into the abyss for its dinner, the remoras will leave it. How sperm whales navigate and feed in the depths of the ocean is a subject of considerable debate.*

The hairs on the upper jaw of this young gray whale are probably sensory and may help it find food or avoid obstacles.

out click trains. Some scientists think they know how it is done. They have proposed that cetaceans can "see" by passive acoustic imaging. Echolocation could be likened to shining a flashlight on a subject in order to view it. Most of the time we do not direct a light at something in order to see it. Sunlight bouncing off an object scatters enough ambient light in our direction for us to form an image of the object. Likewise, plenty of ambient noise is bouncing around in the ocean.

Perhaps enough of this ambient noise can be reflected off an object to enable an animal with a sophisticated sense of hearing to form an image of the object.

An artificial version of such a system was successfully tested in 1994. The device was able to display crude images of large objects from the reflected noises of passing ships, snapping shrimp, and so forth. The inventors believe that in the future submarines will be able to use this sort of sonar without creating noises that could give their position away. Additional research may reveal if whales and dolphins are already using similar technology.

Marine mammals have a tactile sense that, in addition to sensing direct touch, seems to work like the lateral line in fish to detect water displacements. The bristles on the heads of whales and the whiskers on sea lions may function in this capacity, but the details of how this sensory system operates are unknown. Walruses use their facial bristles to feel in the bottom mud for the shellfish they feed on.

SMELL AND TASTE. The lines between smell, taste, and other similar senses are somewhat blurred underwater. Some biologists prefer to lump them all together in the category of chemoreception. Smell and taste are both ways of sampling molecules of a substance by dissolving them onto a sensory membrane. The difference for terrestrial animals such as us is that we use our noses to obtain information about distant objects and our mouths to sample substances that are in contact. We can smell things in very dilute concentrations, but only if the molecules are airborne. In the ocean, scents are all dissolved in seawater and they reach the mouth and nose in the same concentration at the same distance from the source. Because of this

Disadvantaged Snakes

Dissection and examination of their sense organs indicates that sea snakes have poor hearing and little or no sense of taste. It is suspected that they rely on vision and smell to locate their prey. The vision of most appears to be adapted to hunting by daylight, although the eyes of some seem to be well adapted for day and night vision.

One sea snake, *Hydrophis elegans,* has both the most poorly developed visual system of all the sea snakes and the smallest olfactory structures. Scientists examining specimens of this species have concluded that it should have poor hearing, poor vision, and a poor sense of smell. Yet it is fairly widespread around northern Australia and New Guinea and is one of the most common sea snakes in parts of its range. It feeds on moray eels and snake eels—large, dangerous prey items. What senses does it use to capture such difficult prey? And how has it been so successful in spite of its apparent handicaps? Like many marine animals, this species obviously has capabilities that we are not yet able to appreciate.

The expanded nostrils on this blue ribbon eel look like the carburetor scoops on a racing car and function in a similar way—to funnel odor-bearing water through the nostrils and enhance the eel's sense of smell.

some marine animals use taste in the same way that we use smell. Furthermore, many animals have sensory organs apart from their mouths and noses that they use to sample dissolved substances.

Air-breathing marine mammals and reptiles must keep their nostrils closed when they swim, so smelling underwater would seem out of the question. Sea snakes, however, smell with their tongues, which they flick in and out just as land snakes do. No taste buds are on the snake's tongue, but when it is brought back inside the mouth, it is pressed against the Jacobsen's organ. This organ contains nerves leading to the olfactory (smell) lobe of the brain. Seals seem to smell well when they are ashore, but dolphins have apparently lost their sense of smell entirely.

Dolphins were once thought to have only a very crude sense of taste, but more recent observations make it clear that they are very discriminating in their perception of taste. Captive dolphins often show very strong preferences for certain types of fish, and disguising the fish cannot fool them. Wild dolphins have been observed tasting the fecal trails of other dolphins. They are suspected to be able to detect hormones excreted by their companions. On the other hand, biologists are unsure how well developed the sense of taste is in seals and their kin, or if it even exists at all.

Many fish have a very sensitive sense of smell and a correspondingly large olfactory lobe in the brain. This is especially true of sharks, eels, and other predatory fish. Some

sharks can smell blood in the water in concentrations as low as one part per million. Eels can detect some chemicals in concentrations of less than one part in a trillion! Some eels have elaborated external nostrils that apparently gather odors. Most fish have only nostril pits (nares) divided into incoming and outgoing water channels by a flap of skin. Some puffers and a few other fish have no olfactory organs whatsoever and apparently rely completely on sight for feeding.

Moray eels are nocturnal predators with poor vision. They rely mostly upon their superb sense of smell to find prey. The raised tubular nostrils give some indication of the importance of this sense.

A spotted goatfish exerts fine control over its sensory barbels. When the fish is not feeding, the barbels are pulled under the chin and held flat against the body for streamlining.

Bottom-dwelling fishes such as catfish often have taste buds on their skin, fins, and "whiskers." Some codfishes have taste buds on the free rays of their pelvic fins. Goatfish and nurse sharks have chemosensory barbels that they use to probe bottom sediments for food items. So successful are goatfish at locating buried food that they are often accompanied by an entourage of other fish waiting to freeload on whatever the goatfish dig up.

Spiny lobsters use their chemosensory antennules (the smaller antennae beside the large ones) to sample water-borne odors. The large antennae apparently detect water movement, much like the lateral line in fish, and are active organs of defense as well. Spiny lobsters also have chemosensory bristles on the ends of their pointed legs. They can probe bottom sediments with their legs looking for clams, mussels, and other prey. They can both feel and taste a potential food item with their "toes" before deciding whether to dig it up and crack it open.

TURNED ON AND TUNED IN.

A number of aquatic organisms have a sense that humans completely lack, although there are indications that some birds and other terrestrial animals make use of it. This is the electromagnetic sense. Some species of fishes use this "sixth sense" for various purposes, including navigation, communication, finding prey, and detecting nearby objects. It is highly developed

The barbels on the chins of these marine catfish are sensory organs. In this schooling species, they may help the fish orient to each other.

Above: *Electric rays, like this bull's-eye torpedo ray, are strongly electric fish, which use their electricity-generating muscles to stun prey and for self-defense.* Right: *These small pits on the head of a blacktip shark, known as ampullae of Lorenzini, are filled with a jellylike substance and are used to sense electric fields in the water.*

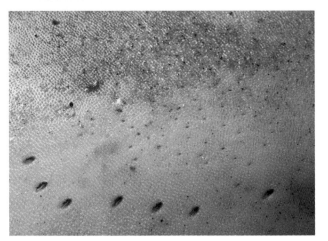

in the sharks and rays. Concentrated on the undersurface of the head in these animals are pit organs called ampullae of Lorenzini, which are filled with electrically conducting gel. With these pit organs, sharks are capable of detecting electric fields as weak as that generated by a flashlight battery connected to terminals 1,000 miles apart in the ocean.

Since muscles are controlled by electrical impulses, all muscled animals create electric fields around them. Even if an animal is lying very still, the contraction of the heart muscles will give it away. Sharks and rays can use their electrical sense to locate prey that is buried under sand and invisible, including each other.

Any electrical conductor moving through a magnetic field generates an electric field. Since the body of a fish is an electrical conductor, an electric field is created around a fish whenever it is swimming across the north-south magnetic field of the earth. The polarity of the field reverses if the fish swims in the opposite direction, and the field disappears if the fish turns 90 degrees and swims parallel to the earth's magnetic lines rather than across them. So a fish with an electrical sense should be able to orient itself to the earth's magnetic field when it swims, just as accurately as if it were holding a compass.

Field experiments have shown that this is exactly what sharks and rays do. Scientists have installed electronic devices in shallow parts of the ocean that enabled them to manipulate the magnetic field over small areas. By twisting the dials, they were able to actually steer sharks and rays swimming through the area.

Seawater itself is an electrical conductor. When ocean currents move across magnetic field lines, they, too, create electric fields. Sharks and rays may therefore also be able to sense tides and currents with their electrical sense.

Some fish generate electricity as well as sense it. Electric rays and stargazers generate strong electric fields used both for defense and, in the ray, for stunning prey. Sea lampreys maintain an electric field

Lampreys belong to a primitive group of fish that branched off from the ancestors of modern fish before the evolution of jaws. Nevertheless, they have some advanced senses, including "electric radar."

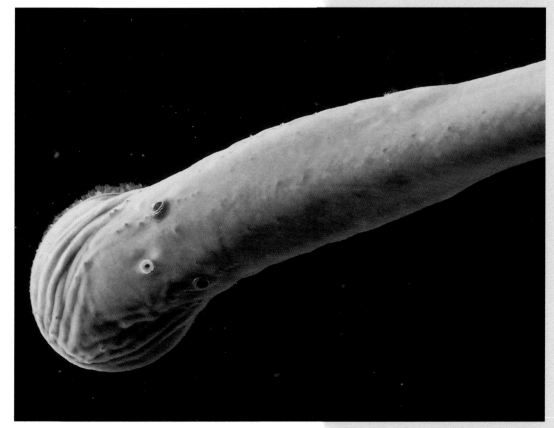

Electrical Attraction

Great hammerhead sharks specialize in feeding on stingrays. They swing their broad, flat heads back and forth across the sea bottom as they scan for electrical signals from beneath the sand, looking like a person using a metal detector to hunt for coins at the beach. Small hammerheads and cat sharks use their electric sense to locate flatfish that bury themselves in the sand, making themselves safe from most other predators.

Even most sharks that hunt in open water use their electric sense in the final moments of an attack. Sensing the low-frequency vibrations of a struggling fish may first alert a shark to the possibility of a meal. As it moves in the direction of the sound, it may begin to pick up the scent trail of the wounded fish, which the shark follows until it makes visual contact. The shark can use its eyesight to move into striking distance and evaluate the condition of the prey. As it moves in for the final attack, the eyes roll back or are covered, and the electrical sensors guide it to its dinner.

Fishermen and filmmakers who have baited sharks in close to their boats have often been surprised—and sometimes alarmed—to see the sharks bite the boat or engine instead of the bait. Some people concluded that sharks are stupid brutes that can't tell the difference between a boat and a mackerel, but in actuality the sharks are merely responding to the electric field created when a metal object is placed in seawater.

Opposite: *A green turtle rests under a coral ledge. Green sea turtles are among the master navigators of the animal world—yet they accomplish their amazing feats with a brain only about the size of a pea!*

around the head, which enables them to sense objects in the dark. If the field is deformed, they know that another object has entered the range of their "radar."

Possibly some of these marine fish also use their electric powers the way freshwater electrical fish, which have been more intensively studied, do. Some freshwater fish maintain a pulsating electric field around their bodies. They use it as lampreys do—to detect prey, predators, or obstacles to be avoided. To get a detailed picture, they can focus a more intense field on the object and examine it, even in murky water in the dark. They use electric signals to communicate with each other, sometimes having "conversations" in which they take turns emitting patterns of electric pulses. They are known to shift frequencies to avoid jamming each other's signals and even to have electric "arguments," directing stronger and stronger bursts of electricity at each other.

INNER MAGNETISM. Some marine animals do not sense electric fields but rather are believed to sense the magnetism of the earth directly, using magnetite crystals in their heads. Magnetite has been found in the heads of various marine animals, including pilot whales, tuna, spiny lobsters, and sea turtles. It is possible that the direct magnetic sense allows more precise navigation than the electric sense. Sea turtles can use their magnetic sense to navigate according to coordinates similar to latitude and longitude.

The seafloor is covered with magnetic anomalies deriving from magnetic patterns created in the bottom rock as it cooled from lava. These deviations from the overall magnetic field of the earth are as distinctive as fingerprints, and they

Magnetite found in the heads of pilot whales suggests that they may be able to use the earth's magnetic field for navigation. Some mass strandings may be caused in part by magnetic anomalies in the seafloor.

can be used to locate a single position over the seafloor even when the bottom cannot be seen. Scalloped hammerhead sharks follow magnetic lines when they migrate between their nighttime feeding areas and the seamounts where they swim during the day.

Scientists have long been baffled by mass strandings, in which large groups of whales or dolphins swim up onto a beach. Suggested explanations include disease, hearing loss (due to parasitic infection, undersea volcanic eruptions, or detonation of explosives, for instance), pollution, and other causes. Each of these is likely involved in some cases. But quite a few of these strandings occur where lines of equal magnetic force that have been running parallel to the coast bend in and touch the coast. It may be that some strandings happen when whales are simply navigating along magnetic lines and fail to make a correction when that line intersects the coastline. Regardless of how strandings occur, many cetaceans are believed to use magnetic information to navigate.

West Indian spiny lobsters make annual migrations in single-file head-to-tail queues. All the queues in the same region tend to move in the same compass direction. Trials with lobsters in tanks where they had no other sources of information showed that they oriented themselves to the earth's magnetic field.

NOTABLE NAVIGATORS. Some

of the migrations of marine animals are nearly miraculous. Probably most involve multiple senses, possibly including some we are not even aware of yet. When a loggerhead turtle hatches at night on the east coast of Florida, it digs its way up out of the

Were these pilot whales fooled by a magnetic field line that turned in toward the coast? Or did they follow an ailing leader to their doom?

2
7
3

A baby loggerhead reaches the ocean after emerging from the nest ashore. It will instinctively swim offshore until it finds floating seaweed in the open ocean where it can hide.

nest in the beach sand and moves instinctively toward the brightest horizon. Under natural conditions, this would be the seaward horizon, since the landward horizon would be obscured by dunes and vegetation. If artificial lights are nearby, the hatchlings may go in the wrong direction and die.

Once it reaches the water, the baby turtle begins to swim against the incoming waves. When it gets past the surf zone, it switches to its magnetic sense to guide it farther out to sea to reach the Gulf Stream current, where it can hide and feed in patches of drifting sargassum. It drifts with the Gulf Stream, following the United States coast north to Nova Scotia, then east with the North Atlantic Drift, cutting south of the British Isles, moving south past the Azores Islands, possibly making an excursion into the Mediterranean, continuing south past the Canary Islands, then crossing westward across the Atlantic again. Eventually the turtle arrives back in Florida, where, with few exceptions, it will breed at exactly the same beach where it hatched perhaps as much as 20 years earlier.

The turtle may continue to migrate between feeding and breeding areas. Divers in Palm Beach, Florida, learned to recognize a very large male loggerhead turtle that appeared on their reefs every year during January and February. They reported finding this individual resting under the exact same ledge on the same reef every year at the same time, give or take one to three weeks. Until very recently, scientists had no idea where the turtles go between hatching and returning as adults or sub-adults. They still are not sure exactly how they find their way home.

MASTERS OF MIGRATION.

Salmon are legendary migrators. From their native streams on the west coast of North America, some of them cross the North Pacific almost to Japan and spend several years at sea before returning to their home stream to breed. They use their extraordinary sense of smell and equally remarkable memory to identify the mouth of their home river. Then they follow their smell upstream, almost always choosing the correct branch to finally arrive at the headwaters of the tributary where they hatched from the egg. Chemicals dissolved from soil, rocks, and vegetation give each stream a unique olfactory signature, which is imprinted in the salmon's brain at a very early age. But can this sense guide them across the open ocean to reach the correct spot on the coast? Many investigators think not. They feel confident that salmon will be found to be using magnetic or other navigational tools during the open ocean part of their migration.

Turtles Without Pensions

For pinpoint accuracy, little can match the feat of the green turtles that nest at Ascension Island, a five-mile-long speck of land in the middle of the South Atlantic Ocean. During World War II, finding the Ascension Island refueling station was a critical test of an aircraft navigator's ability. "If you miss Ascension, your wife gets a pension," was the grim reminder. Yet at the onset of breeding season, a large number of the adult green sea turtles feeding in the sea-grass pastures along the coast of Brazil head across the Atlantic to Ascension, where the shore is completely barren and there is nothing for them to eat. After mating and laying eggs, they make the 1,400-mile return trip to South America to resume feeding.

How do they find it? Could they be looking at the stars when they come to the surface to breathe? Not likely: Sea turtles see well underwater but are quite nearsighted in air. Not to mention that the stars are not visible by day or during cloudy periods. Are they listening to the sounds of waves striking the island, or snapping shrimp on the narrow ledges around it, or undersea volcanoes at its base? Possibly, but the eardrums of sea turtles are covered with skin, and they apparently hear best at low frequencies. Do they smell or taste the vegetation on the island as they approach it? Likely, but probably only when they are most of the way there. They certainly use their magnetic sense, but almost certainly need others as well to make the precise landfall.

Above: *Female elephant seals molt at the same beach where they breed at a different time of year. Each year they travel back and forth from the feeding grounds twice—once to molt and once to breed. Right: A mudskipper goby rests at the edge of a tide pool. If the tide pool dries up, the goby will have to go to another. Opposite: On most rocky shorelines the retreating tide leaves pools of water. Mudskipper gobies live in these pools and jump from one to another as they start to dry up, sometimes accurately jumping into a pool it cannot see.*

Salmon make their great migration only once in their lives, but some marine mammals make amazing journeys every year. Gray whales may travel more than 10,000 miles round-trip between feeding and breeding grounds each year. Elephant seals complete two long-distance migrations each year. From their offshore feeding areas they swim thousands of miles to the breeding beaches, swim back out to sea to feed some more, and then return to the beach later in the year to molt. The total mileage for both trips can exceed 13,000.

MAPS AND CLOCKS.

The amazing homing abilities of many animals require that they have some sort of internal map sense that gives them an understanding of the spatial relationships between features of their environment. Such a map sense is clearly demonstrated by certain gobies— small fish that live in tide pools. Some of them jump from pool to pool as the tide goes out and their pool starts to dry up. Often they can't see the pool they will jump into from the one that they are in. And these may

A queen conch peers out of its shell with eyes held on stalks. In some mollusks and crustaceans, the eyestalks have been found to serve as hormone-secreting glands as well as visual organs, and they may contain the internal clock that regulates the organism's metabolism and reproductive cycle.

be quite small pools surrounded by large areas of exposed rock. Yet the gobies always land in a pool when they jump. To know exactly which direction to jump to land in water, they must form a map of where all of the basins are. Probably they do this at high tide when they can swim around freely.

Many migrations and other activities require, along with a map sense for direction, a clock sense for timing. Various animals, of course, take advantage of environmental cues to tell them when to undertake certain activities. But in some

cases no adequate cues are available to explain the accuracy of their timing. And animals taken into laboratories and deprived of day-night light cycles and other stimuli often continue to exhibit their daily behaviors at regular intervals. These intervals correspond to the rhythms of tides, daylight, and/or the lunar and solar calendars. Some animals may have more than one internal clock running simultaneously. The internal clocks that time these rhythms are genetically controlled. The clocks are located in the eyestalks of some mollusks and crustaceans, in the brains of some other animals, and throughout the entire body of at least one seaweed (an alga). The alga can be cut into pieces less than half an inch long, and each piece will continue to exhibit daily rhythms in its metabolism.

The internal clocks will lose their accuracy if not continually adjusted according to input from the environment. This combination can result in remarkably accurate coordination of natural events. The annual spawning of star corals in the Western Atlantic and Gulf of Mexico can be predicted within about 15

A colony of star coral sends a cloud of gametes into the night ocean at precisely the same time as hundreds of other colonies in the area.

The pink egg-shaped capsules released by a spawning star coral are not actually eggs but packets containing a large number of small eggs and sperm. The eggs are not fertilized by sperm from the same coral, though. Apparently they can detect the sperm's chemical signature and block fertilization.

minutes, based on the solar and lunar calendars. It occurs at the same time over large areas of ocean. The environmental cues the corals use to set their internal clocks have not been fully identified, but water temperature, daylight, moonlight, and/or tidal periods are suspected to play a part. The great mystery is how the corals detect any of these factors.

PASSING MESSAGES. Some natural events require additional coordination by communication between the organisms involved. Many types of sponges spawn at about the same time each year, and mostly around certain phases of the moon, but their spawning cannot be predicted as precisely as that of star corals. When the environmental conditions are about right, one sponge begins to spawn. As its gametes drift down-current, they reach other sponges and trigger these to spawn as well.

Chemical communication like this is used by many animals to coordinate reproductive activities, to warn of predators, and to convey other messages. Many

Since sponges, such as this giant barrel sponge, spend their lives attached to the same spot on the reef, they must do their "dating" by long distance, using chemical signals to coordinate spawning times.

tunicates, or sea squirts, use chemicals to recognize which other sea squirts are relatives and which are from a different genetic stock. If they recognize the scent of their own genetic stock, encroaching tunicates will be allowed to join the colony. If they smell a stranger, toxic chemicals will be used to drive the invaders off.

Marine animals use many other methods to exchange information. Several types of fishes use sound to convey a number of different meanings. Groupers

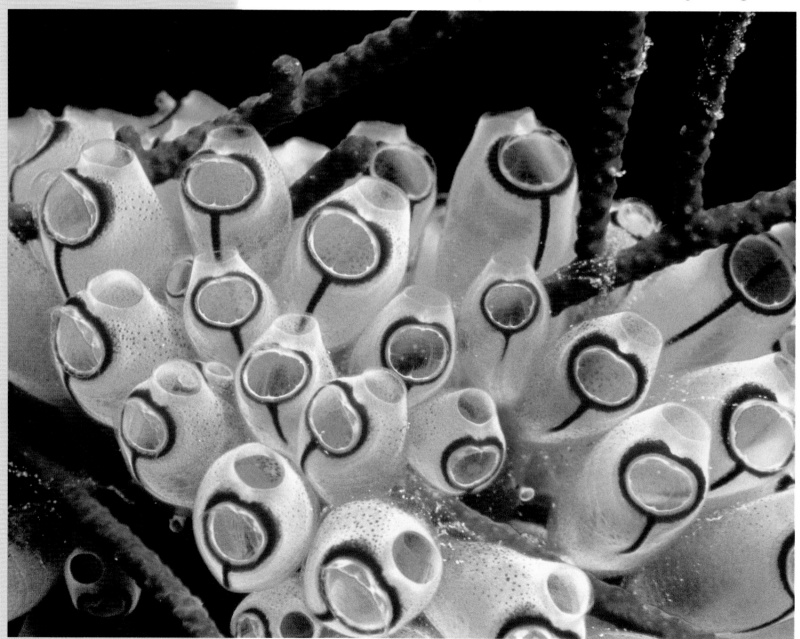

A cluster of painted tunicates clings to a purple gorgonian (soft coral). Some types of tunicates have been shown to recognize the chemical "fingerprint" of other tunicates.

A bouquet of multicolored tunicate colonies all competing for space on a coral reef. If genetically identical colonies touch, they may fuse to form a single colony. But if a colony contacts an unrelated colony, it will attack with chemical weapons.

vibrate their air bladders to make a loud boom that warns other fish away from their territory. Male bicolor damselfish make a single chirp before attacking an intruder; two chirps when readying themselves to spawn; three chirps to signal females that they are ready to mate; four to five chirps when a female approaches the nest but tries to leave without spawning; and other sounds while in the nest.

Spiny lobsters rasp the bases of their antennae against ribbed pads in the antennae's sockets to make a distress squeak. Stone crabs rub the tip of a claw against a

Disturbing Communications

In spring, along the coast of California, the males of a type of toadfish known as a midshipman advertise for females with a noise that sounds something like a boat whistle. To create this sound, the fish contracts and relaxes its swim-bladder muscle at a rate of 200 times per second—more than twice the frequency of a diamondback rattlesnake's rattle. This is the highest-frequency muscular contraction measured in any vertebrate. The sound is loud, carries a long distance, and can be heard out of the water.

Around marinas, where people are living on boats, the fish are common. Their calls transmit well through boat hulls, disturbing the sleep of the occupants. Every spring, without fail, numbers of people living on boats along the West Coast come to their own conclusions about the sources of the disturbance and make complaints about "secret Navy experiments" and other presumed causes.

Above: *Sea horses make noises when investigating new features in their environment, but the significance of the noises is not known.* Opposite: *A manatee's vocal repertoire appears limited in comparison to that of more social animals.*

ridged area on the opposite claw to make a variety of rasping noises. Nobody knows what they are "saying" to each other. Sea horses make little pops when exploring new situations. Gobies "snore" in response to trespassers in their territories. Snapping shrimp snap, grunts grunt, and gray angelfish moan. The so-called "Silent World" is full of the noises of animals communicating with one another.

Marine mammals, with their extraordinary sonic capabilities, make extensive use of acoustic communications, but little is known about what sort of information is being exchanged. Walruses make mysterious gonglike sounds, whereas manatees make a variety of high-pitched squeals. Female manatees use individually distinctive high-pitched squeals to summon their calves underwater. While onshore, seals and sea lions make distinctive bleats by which mothers and calves recognize each other.

Whales and dolphins have the most elaborate repertoire of calls. Belugas, or white whales, are known as "canaries of the sea" for their lively chatter. On

their breeding grounds, male humpback whales sing intricate songs for hours. Other sounds are exchanged between courting couples, mothers and calves, individuals in a cooperative feeding group, and in other situations.

To human observers blue whales seem to pass by in stately silence, but this is only because their communication channel is below the threshold of human hearing. Low-frequency sounds carry farther in water. Scientists now believe that blue whales can communicate with each other across an entire ocean and perhaps from anywhere in the world.

SOUNDS OF MEANING. Dolphins use both ultrasound and infrasound as

well as an amazing variety of sounds that we can hear. But what does it all mean? A distinctive squawk made while shaking the head up and down and baring the

Opposite: *Belugas are curious and gregarious whales that communicate with a near-constant chatter of whistles, trills, clicks, and warbles. The noises are so loud that they can often be heard in air. Below: A coalition of spotted dolphins warns off another group with loud squawking accompanied by head shaking and an open-mouth display revealing the teeth. If the other dolphins do not heed the warning, the display may escalate into open aggression including tooth rakes and body slams.*

Opposite: *Breaching is one of the most spectacular displays in the animal kingdom. A variety of reasons may cause this 40-ton humpback whale to exert the energy to propel itself out of the water.*

teeth is an unmistakable threat, as is an equally unambiguous signal called a jaw pop or jaw clap, which sounds almost like a gun being fired. Each dolphin has a unique signature whistle that identifies it to other members of the group. This sound can be modulated to add emotional characteristics to the identifying call. Dolphins sometimes use each other's signature whistles, perhaps to call or address each other. But do all the other sounds add up to a language?

Researchers have shown that both sea lions and dolphins have the cognitive ability to understand language. Both types of animals have learned artificial languages in captivity and have demonstrated an ability to understand syntax (relationship between word order and meaning) and master fairly lengthy sentences. But no one can say if either animal has a true language that it uses in the wild. Certainly many types of information can be conveyed with different sounds.

One of the functions of breaching, or leaping, is almost certainly to make a loud noise to signal other whales or dolphins. The sound of a

whale crashing back into the water after a spectacular breach is sometimes answered by another whale breaching, often miles away. The two may continue the conversation for dozens of breaches, alternating from one whale to the other.

But some people have proposed that dolphins can generate sound patterns that re-create the echoes they receive when using their "sonar." By directing these sounds to another dolphin, they suggest, a dolphin can transmit a three-dimensional sonic image of something it has "seen" or perhaps imagined. Biologists are mostly skeptical, but the possibility has not been ruled out.

GESTURES. Whales and dolphins also communicate by touch and by body language, techniques almost universal in the animal kingdom. An open mouth is a threat. Creatures signal each other by body posture or position or movements of body parts. Some of the body parts have been modified through evolution, making them more effective as signaling devices. Dolphins often pat each other with their pectoral fins in what seems to be a sign of reassurance. Sometimes the mutual pats go on for a long time and seem to be carrying perhaps more complex messages, almost like Morse code.

The threat posture of a crab with claws raised is unmistakable in its meaning. But the crab claw can communicate many other things. Male fiddler crabs, which live on sand or in mudflats exposed at low tide, have one greatly enlarged and brightly colored claw. They use it to make signals related to courtship and territorial defense. The large claw is not used for feeding; its only function is communication. Each population of fiddler crab appears to have its own dialect of sign language. For a few populations that have been

Speaking a Foreign Language

One type of shrimp, which shares coral heads with a type of crab, has learned to "speak" that crab's body language. The small crabs live on branching corals in the Indo-Pacific, feeding on coral mucus and on particles trapped by the mucus. The crabs aggressively drive off intruders from their coral head, including members of their own species, unless the intruder is a crab of the opposite sex. When a crab of the opposite sex is encountered, the pair defuse aggression by making appeasement signals that consist of gently touching or rubbing the other crab's shell or claws. When a snapping shrimp enters a crab's territory, it makes the same appeasement signals that a crab of the opposite sex would make. These signals induce the crab to accept the less powerful shrimp and allow it to stay on the coral head. The signals are never used by shrimp with each other, so they are considered to be "crab-ese."

studied, "dictionaries" have been published with drawings of claw postures and explanations of their meanings.

Many fish raise and lower fins to send messages to other fish. In a number of kinds of blennies, the dorsal fin has been expanded into a large semaphore signal. Since the blennies mostly live in holes and do little swimming, the only function of the enlarged fin appears to be for communication. Gray reef sharks

The body language of this crab is un-mistakable. It says, "You are threatening me. If you come closer, I will pinch you with my claws!"

This Nassau grouper exhibits its normal banded color pattern. Living alone in its territory, it has no need or opportunity to communicate with other members of its species. But at spawning time, when many groupers gather together, different color patterns appear as the fish pass messages back and forth.

signal aggression with an exaggerated S-shaped body posture. Divers who failed to heed a shark's warning have been seriously injured when the shark made good on its threat.

VISUAL SIGNS.

Especially in coral reef fish, color patterns often carry messages. These patterns may be fixed throughout the life of the fish, may change as the fish grows or ages, may change seasonally (during breeding, for example), or may be under the fish's control to change instantly. Nassau groupers keep a constant pattern during most of the year, but they exhibit a variety of color patterns during the breeding season. For only one of these patterns is the meaning understood—the one that indicates spawning is imminent. Some unicorn fish blush blue-white when courting, whereas some jacks go black and bicolor damselfish may gain a golden "crown."

Emperor angelfish have one very striking color pattern as juveniles and another equally flamboyant pattern as adults. It appears that the patterns may

An adult emperor angelfish displays a bold warning color pattern. Adults will attack wooden models painted with the adult pattern much more frequently than models carrying the juvenile pattern, even if the "adult" model is small and the "juvenile" model is large.

serve to help the angelfish space themselves out on the reef to assure an adequate food supply for each fish. If an adult angelfish spots another adult color pattern in its territory, it will attack and chase the intruder. But since the juveniles do not compete for the same food as the adults, they carry different color patterns, which are tolerated by the adults.

Indo-Pacific cleaner wrasses also exhibit separate color patterns for juveniles and adults, to protect the juveniles from adult aggression. Juveniles will switch to the adult coloration if no adults are present but switch back to the juvenile coloration if placed with adult fish.

Fish manufacture some of the pigments they use to color themselves, but they obtain others from plants in their diet. Just as human artists often prepare a canvas with a coat of white to give a brighter appearance to the colors added later, fish often have a layer of reflective white guanine crystals in some of their pigment cells. The guanine crystals can be arranged to diffract, reflect, and scatter light in different ways to create colors for which the fish have no pigments, such as blue, which seems to

Talking Colors

Cephalopods, like fish, use color patterns to communicate with each other. But, with more sophisticated nervous control of the pigment cells in their skin, cephalopods are able to produce a greater variety of intricate skin patterns and to transmit more complex messages. Squid, which tend to live in groups, may have the most developed color pattern "language." They exhibit various color patterns during courtship, during aggressive encounters with other squid, and as warnings when predators approach.

Caribbean reef squid, upon sighting a predator, exhibit a pattern that not only warns the other squid of danger but may actually identify the specific type of predator. They can even carry on two "conversations" at once. A researcher once spotted a male squid approaching a female showing a courtship display on the side of its body facing the female and simultaneously displaying an aggressive pattern toward another male on the other side.

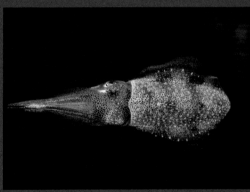

Caribbean reef squid, taken seconds apart

Most cephalopods can see polarized light, but cuttlefish are actually able to arrange the reflector cells in their skin to reflect light in polarized patterns, which they use to communicate with other cuttlefish. The polarized patterns seem to be used mostly in aggressive displays.

Opposite: The color pattern of this juvenile emperor angelfish is strikingly different from that of the adult.

A big-eye snapper (above) can change its color pattern in an instant. The red color (opposite) might seem to be a disadvantage, but this is a nocturnal fish, which normally stays in dark caverns during the day. Without artificial light, its red hue is not visible in the darkness.

be a difficult pigment for most fish to make. Cephalopods use the same trick to add blue to their palette.

Many fish, shrimp, and other animals that are active at night or live in deep water are colored red. This seems baffling, since their red color is not visible without artificial light. But this is exactly why they have this color. Red appears gray or black in the absence of red light, providing concealment for these animals in low light. Red color in the outer layers of the skin may actually be superior to gray for masking underlying patterns.

QUICK STUDIES. Marine animals, like those on land, not only communicate with each other but learn from each other. Marine mammals are especially well known for their ability to copy new behaviors and skills from each other. Some experiments have suggested that dolphins can use vocalizations to instruct a

companion how to solve a problem, but these results are ambiguous. Dolphins can definitely learn by watching. Their quick learning ability has not endeared dolphins or sea lions to fishermen. Fishermen have learned that once one of these animals discovers how to steal fish from their gear, the knowledge spreads rapidly through the population.

Cephalopods have the most complex brains of any invertebrates. In laboratory experiments, octopuses that watched an animal in a neighboring aquarium solve a problem were able to solve it themselves in a fraction of the time it took "untutored" animals. The most famous demonstration of the intelligence of octopuses was observed only accidentally when a scientist stopped by the lab after

Octopuses are typically seen crawling on the bottom, but they can also swim, using a form of jet propulsion, by forcing water through their funnels. Some types of octopus spend their entire lives in the open ocean.

hours. For some time, the staff had been baffled by the mysterious disappearance of fish from tanks at the facility. The nighttime inspection revealed that an octo-pus was leaving its tank at night, lifting the lid of a fish tank to gain entrance, eating the occupants, replac-ing the lid, retreating to its own tank, and then replacing its own lid to escape detection. Many other events have demonstrated the problem-solving ability and quick learning capacity of cephalo-pods. What remains unanswered is why these learning skills evolved in animals with such short life spans— one to a few years. Normally, short-lived animals operate mostly on instinct, while animals with longer life spans are able to put to use what they learn from experience.

Sea turtles, on the other hand, live longer, grow larger, and belong to a "higher" group of animals, but have brains about the size of a pea. A turtle spe-cialist once presented a talk on "The Evolutionary Advantages of Being Stupid." Even so, the navigational abilities of turtles are nothing short of miraculous.

Some loggerhead turtles make an-nual migrations, returning each year to favored reefs with astonish-ing accuracy. Particles of magnetite in their brains probably work like a compass to detect the earth's mag-netic field.

The Final Frontier

For those who wish to challenge the unknown, the sea is the final frontier. Recent discoveries have revealed entirely new kinds of animals and changed our understanding of how life works. And yet we have just begun to explore the deep ocean, which covers most of the planet. Undoubtedly new discoveries will reveal facts even more incredible than those that have already been uncovered. In 1960 scientists were astounded to discover that some of the very earliest life-forms that existed on

The Great Blue Hole of Belize is, for many people, a symbol of the mystery of the oceans. It is still only partially explored.

Earth—found in fossils 3½ billion years old—were still around and growing in the ocean. These were rocklike structures known as stromatolites, formed by bacteria and algae. They were found in shallow habitats in western Australia and later in the Bahamas as well. Some scientists likened it to finding a living dinosaur. Some of the individual structures are more than 1,000 years old, growing at a rate of about ½₅ inch a year.

Hydrothermal vents were discovered in 1977 at depths of almost two miles, where the warm water nourished fantastic gardens of strange animals growing in incredible profusion at these undersea oases. Up until this time all life on earth was believed to depend ultimately upon photosynthesis powered by the energy of sunlight. However, the animals living around the vents were found to be feeding on bacteria that derived their energy from chemosynthesis—chemical energy released from hydrogen sulfide and other substances spewed from the vents. We suddenly had to accept a whole new notion of how life operates.

In 1984 similar communities were found at depths of less than half a mile on top of salt domes in the Gulf of Mexico, where the bacteria were getting their energy from methane and hydrogen sulfide released from natural petroleum seeps. It now appears that chemosynthesis may not

This view from a deep-sea submersible shows the community of tube worms, clams, and other creatures living around a hydrothermal vent, where hot water is released from a volcanic rift miles below the surface of the ocean.

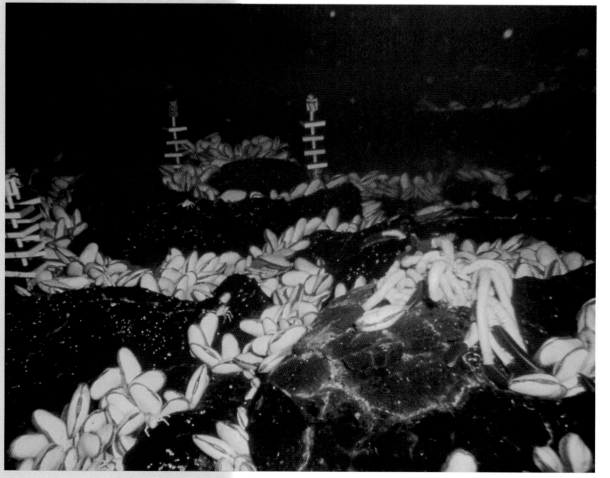

be that unusual in the ocean—and may affect the energy balance of the entire planet.

A research vessel working off the Hawaiian Islands in 1976 had some difficulty retrieving a sea anchor. When it was finally pulled up, a 15-foot-long shark was stuck on it. The shark had a huge mouth with small teeth and was quite unlike anything that had ever been seen before. A new family had to be created in order to classify the sea monster, which was dubbed Megamouth. A live specimen was not observed until 1989, and not until 1994 was the first female seen.

THE DEPTH OF OUR IGNORANCE.
Each unique type of organism belongs to a species. Closely related species are grouped together in a genus. A family usually contains more than one genus. The next larger group above family is class, followed by order, with phylum as the broadest type of classification for animals. The phylum Chordata, for example, includes mammals, fishes, amphibians, reptiles, and birds. Even in well-visited areas such as coral reefs, our knowledge is still so sparse that a specialist in a particular group of marine animals often has no trouble finding new species on a collecting trip. To discover a new genus is not that unusual. To find, with the Megamouth discovery, a whole new family of sharks was quite exciting. To discover a new class of organisms is for a biologist almost an impossible dream.

The giant Megamouth shark was not discovered until 1976, and only about six specimens have ever been found. The shark pictured is the only member of its kind ever to have been seen alive.

Yet in 1980 divers in a flooded cave in the Bahamas discovered some small crustaceans, which they named remipedes. They turned out to belong to a whole new class. In 1995 researchers in Norway found tiny organisms living on the lips of lobsters. These organisms were so strange they had to placed in a new phylum.

Classes and phyla (plural of phylum) are the largest categories of animal life. So here, at the end of the 20th century, we are still discovering the basic structures of the animal kingdom and still revising our view of what are the necessary conditions for life. And our knowledge of the biology and natural history of most forms of ocean life is minimal, even for those marine animals that are quite familiar. Since the largest fish in the ocean often swims at the surface and is easily approached by boats and divers, you might think that we know all about it. But no one knows where whale sharks mate and give birth, why they suddenly appear at certain places at certain times, or where they go the rest of the time. Nobody knows how many there are, or how much they are being affected by fishing and other human activities. Until 1996 no one knew if they laid eggs or gave live birth, or how many offspring they might have. It was then that a female whale shark was caught with 300 live embryos inside her—about 30 times as many as were expected.

A remipede looks like a segmented worm, but it is more closely related to a shrimp. The discovery of these organisms living in caves in the Bahamas required the creation of a new scientific class to hold them. A class is the second highest category of animal life.

DISCOVERY IN THE DEEP WATER.

In the past most of the information about life in the deep sea was gained by pulling it up with nets and dredges. These methods miss anything that is active enough to get out of the way. And what is pulled up is often mangled beyond recognition. When scientists began to dive deep with large-window submersibles and to send down remotely operated video cameras to observe deep-sea life in its own habitat, they discovered a whole world of strange new organisms; things like *Vampyroteuthis infernalis*. This big-eyed squid, whose scientific name means "the vampire squid from Hell," rolls up into a spiky ball when threatened. They found that sea cucumbers, which exist in shallow habitats as sluglike bottom-feeders, have deep-sea varieties that undulate through the open ocean with the grace of ballerinas.

Those who feel that we have already learned all there is to know about our planet have only to look beneath the surface of the waves. There they will find a world of mystery waiting for our discovery.

Only in 1996 did scientists finally learn how the whale shark, the largest fish in the sea, reproduces.